Gail - 154.44.
Aherns - 152.22.
Hidalgo - 72
Joanne - Pesca #10
610.619.3506

CULTURE SMART!

MEXICO

Guy Mavor

Hane - $ 3810

·K·U·P·E·R·A·R·D·

First published in Great Britain 2005
by Kuperard, an imprint of Bravo Ltd
59 Hutton Grove, London N12 8DS
Tel: +44 (0) 20 8446 2440   Fax: +44 (0) 20 8446 2441
www.culturesmartguides.com
Inquiries: sales@kuperard.co.uk

Culture Smart! is a registered trademark of Bravo Ltd

Distributed in the United States and Canada
by Random House Distribution Services
1745 Broadway, New York, NY 10019
Tel: +1 (212) 572-2844   Fax: +1 (212) 572-4961
Inquiries: csorders@randomhouse.com

Copyright © 2005 Kuperard

Second printing (revised) 2006

Series Editor Geoffrey Chesler

ISBN-13: 978 1 85733 366 4
ISBN-10: 1 85733 366 7

British Library Cataloguing in Publication Data
A CIP catalogue entry for this book is available from the
British Library

Printed in Malaysia

This book is available for special discounts for bulk purchases for
sales promotions or premiums. Special editions, including
personalized covers, excerpts of existing books, and corporate
imprints, can be created in large quantities for special needs.

For more information in the U.S.A. write to Special
Markets/Premium Sales, 1745 Broadway, MD 6–2, New York,
NY 10019 or e-mail specialmarkets@randomhouse.com.

In the United Kingdom contact Kuperard publishers at the
above address.

Cover image: Woven cloth, Kava.
Travel Ink/Kevin Nicol

CultureSmart!Consulting and **Culture Smart!** guides have both
contributed to and featured regularly in the weekly travel program
"Fast Track" on BBC World TV.

About the Author

GUY MAVOR is a writer and journalist currently based in London. He graduated from the University of Bristol in 1998 with a BA Hons in French and Spanish, specializing in Mexican history and literature. Since then, he has traveled, researched, and written extensively about his experience of other cultures, ancient and modern, for both television and travel publishers. Guy has lived and worked in a number of countries across the globe, including France, Spain, Mexico, and South Africa. He is coauthor of *The Greenwood Guide to South Africa*.

Other Books in the Series

- Culture Smart! Argentina
- Culture Smart! Australia
- Culture Smart! Belgium
- Culture Smart! Brazil
- Culture Smart! Britain
- Culture Smart! China
- Culture Smart! Costa Rica
- Culture Smart! Cuba
- Culture Smart! Czech Republic
- Culture Smart! Denmark
- Culture Smart! Finland
- Culture Smart! France
- Culture Smart! Germany
- Culture Smart! Greece
- Culture Smart! Hong Kong
- Culture Smart! Hungary
- Culture Smart! India
- Culture Smart! Ireland
- Culture Smart! Italy
- Culture Smart! Japan
- Culture Smart! Korea
- Culture Smart! Morocco
- Culture Smart! Netherlands
- Culture Smart! New Zealand
- Culture Smart! Norway
- Culture Smart! Panama
- Culture Smart! Peru
- Culture Smart! Philippines
- Culture Smart! Poland
- Culture Smart! Portugal
- Culture Smart! Russia
- Culture Smart! Singapore
- Culture Smart! Spain
- Culture Smart! Sweden
- Culture Smart! Switzerland
- Culture Smart! Thailand
- Culture Smart! Turkey
- Culture Smart! Ukraine
- Culture Smart! USA
- Culture Smart! Vietnam

Other titles are in preparation. For more information, contact: info@kuperard.co.uk

The publishers would like to thank **CultureSmart!**Consulting for its help in researching and developing the concept for this series.

contents

contents

Map of Mexico

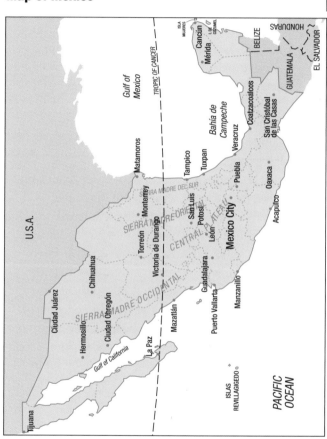

introduction

In the popular imagination, Mexico conjures
up images of ancient civilizations, plundering
conquistadores, and mustachioed revolutionaries.
More penetrating insights are provided by figures
such as the artistic colossus Diego Rivera and
Nobel Prize-winning writer, poet, and
philosopher Octavio Paz. But there is really no
substitute for being there and experiencing
Mexico for oneself.

The many contradictions of this vibrant land
are reflected in the character of the people.
Mexicans are intensely fatalistic, resigned even. But
when the mood takes them, they are hedonistic
and carefree. Likewise, a reserved, poker-faced
demeanor will suddenly, once you get to know
someone, give way to astonishing warmth and
familiarity. The country's first hundred years of
independence were spectacularly bloody, yet it has
been at peace for eighty-five years. It shares a long
land border with its northern neighbor, yet it
could not be more different.

The explanation lies in Mexico's unique
history. Five hundred years ago, two previously
separate branches of humanity collided in the
central Mexican highlands, and the clash
reverberates strongly even now. Spain brought

Catholicism to Mexico, but its missionaries took a pragmatic approach and incorporated earlier religious beliefs. The defining Mexican festival is known as *Día de los Muertos, Hanal Pixan,* or the Day of the Dead; it merges All Saints' and All Souls' Days with indigenous death rituals, and is unlike Catholic celebrations of these feast days anywhere else in the world.

Mexico has emerged from this dual and bloody history to claim its place in the modern world. Today globalization and free trade are altering Mexican society once again. However, the Mexicans have yet to embrace consumerism as a way of life; they still seem to rely on human relationships (the family is paramount) for their happiness.

Culture Smart! Mexico introduces you to the complex realities of modern Mexican life. It describes how history has shaped Mexicans' values and attitudes, and reveals what they are like at home, work, and play. The chapter on customs and traditions gives a flavor of religious and public life, while those on meeting people and "time out" will help you to make the most of your visit. Mexicans value human contact highly—the more effort you make to meet and understand people, the more you will enjoy your stay.

Key Facts

Official Name	Estados Unidos Mexicanos (United Mexican States)	
Capital City	Ciudad de México (Mexico City)	Population approx. 22 million
System of Government	Federal Republic with an elected President serving a six-year term	Two legislative chambers
Population	Approx. 100 million	
Area	756,066 sq. miles (1,958,201 sq. km)	
Geography	Long border with U.S.A. to north, and with Guatemala and Belize to south	Two-thirds of the country lie within the tropics.
Terrain	Great diversity of landscapes: incl. Pacific and Caribbean coastlines, large central plateau, snowcapped mountain ranges, desert in north, and jungle in south and east	The low-lying Yucatán peninsula extends east into the Caribbean.
Climate	Hugely varied. Coastlines and lowlands hot and humid	Highlands and far northwest coast more temperate
Currency	The peso. Divides into 100 centavos	
GDP Per Capita	US $3,700	
Life Expectancy	Men 68 years, women 75 years	

Ethnic Makeup	Mostly mixed European and Indian	Approximately sixty indigenous groups, mainly in the south
Language	Spanish is the official language.	Indigenous languages such as Nahuatl and Maya are spoken widely at local level.
Religion	Around 90% Roman Catholic	
Adult Literacy Rate	89%	
Press	Each state has own, mostly uncritical, regional newspaper.	The independent national press incl. the left-wing *La Jornada* and the newer *Reforma*.
Television	TV dominated by *telenovelas* (soap operas)	Cable and satellite throughout urban areas
English Media	English-language newspapers are limited. Free English bulletins from urban newsstands; also news magazines	US cable channels widely available
Electricity	110 volts, 60 Hz A/C (same as U.S.A.)	European plugs need adaptors.
Video/TV	NTSC system	
Telephone	Mexico's country code is 52. Each main city area has an extra two digits. Cell phone numbers start with 044.	To dial out of Mexico, dial 00; to dial between states dial 01.
Time	GMT minus 4–8 hours (more the farther west)	

chapter one

LAND &
PEOPLE

A GEOGRAPHICAL SNAPSHOT

Mexico is the smallest and most southerly of the three huge countries that make up North America, the other two being Canada and the United States of America. It shares a long northern border (1,933 miles/3,110 km) with the U.S.A., and shorter borders with Guatemala and Belize to the south and southeast respectively. Mexico is a Spanish-speaking country with just over 100 million inhabitants, 22 million of whom live in the vast, sprawling capital, Mexico City.

Within Mexico is a huge variety of landscapes: tropical, palm-fringed coastlines, snowcapped mountains rising to 17,000 ft (5,200 m) and beyond, active volcanoes (the country is situated on a geological fault line and earthquakes are also frequent), desert in the north, jungle in the south and east, and coniferous forests in the central highlands. The flat, low-lying Yucatán peninsula stretches out into the Caribbean to the east, while two long mountain ranges dominate the rest of the country. The Sierra Madre runs the length of Mexico, and continues the line begun by the Rocky Mountains to the north, although split into two ranges. The Sierra Madres Oriental and Occidental, respectively in the east and west of the country, are separated by a fertile central plateau.

When such a mountainous interior is combined with a tropical latitude, rainfall will inevitably follow, and there is an abundance of rivers and large lakes across Mexico. Most major watercourses flow into the sea, though some drain into inland lakes such as Lake Chapala (in Jalisco state), the country's largest. Mexico's longest river, the Río Bravo (known as the Rio Grande in the U.S.A.), forms the border with Texas to the north.

Mexico also has 7,245 miles (11,592 km) of coastline, not including its coastal islands. The Pacific, or western, coastline is dominated by cliffs and rapidly rising landscapes, while the Gulf coast is mostly flat, with long, sandy beaches.

CLIMATE

Mexico's climate is inextricably linked to its physical geography. Two-thirds of the country lie within the tropics, roughly on the same latitude as "the southernmost tip of Hawaii . . . or very much further east, the town of Juggernaut in India, on the Bay of Bengal," as Malcolm Lowry put it in the opening chapter of his brilliant novel *Under the Volcano*. On the coast, in the flat expanse of the Yucatán peninsula and along the Gulf of Mexico and most of the Pacific coastline, there is no mistaking the tropical latitude. Only the northwest coast escapes the heat and humidity.

The interior, however, is largely temperate. The high central plateau tempers the latitude with altitude. Whereas in the Yucatán the weather varies from hot and humid to hot and humid with a chance of hurricane (the season is August to December), the seasonal changes in the central plateau are more pronounced, with winter cooler and drier, and summer warmer and wetter.

Desert in the far north of the country and thick jungle in the far south also reflect the fact that rainfall increases dramatically as you move south into the tropical belt.

THE STATES OF MEXICO

Mexico, a Federal Republic, is divided into thirty-one states and one Federal District, incorporating the capital city. The most heavily populated is

Mexico state, which contains the spillover
population from the Federal District, which itself
has the second-largest population, even though it
covers by far the smallest area of any state.
Generally speaking, the vast and relatively arid
northern states are less densely populated than
those in the south, and neither of these two regions
are as populous as the historical heart of Mexico,
the fertile central valleys between the two Sierras.

A BRIEF HISTORY

Modern Mexico has emerged from a number of
disparate historical currents. These, as the heading
suggests, can only be covered in the briefest of
detail here. But you cannot ignore any of them if
you are looking to understand the country and its
people. Whereas many nations in the New World
have either forgotten or deliberately discarded
their pre-Columbian pasts, Mexico's is impossible
to avoid. The word "Mexico"
itself derives from the Mexica
tribe, who laid the foundations
for the Aztec empire, the
sophisticated civilization
encountered by Spanish *conquistadores* in the
early sixteenth century. After the conquest, Spain
built its own empire in Mexico, and its buildings
can be seen alongside, and in many cases on top

of, those of earlier civilizations. Since independence, foreign powers have held varying degrees of influence over the country, though none, not even the economic and cultural leviathan to the north, have managed to dilute or significantly alter Mexico's essence and identity. In these days of global treaties and NAFTA, however, anything is possible.

Prehistory

The first evidence of settlement in what is now Mexico, involving agriculture, basic pottery, and the use of rudimentary tools, dates from around 5000 BCE. Before then the country, along with the rest of the Americas, was peopled by nomadic Stone Age hunter-gatherers, whose ancestors crossed the Bering Strait in waves and gradually migrated southward from around 13,000 BCE until the end of the last ice age around 6000 BCE.

Mesoamerican Civilizations

The term "Mesoamerica" literally means Middle America, and is no more than a geographical description. However, it takes on extra meaning when combined with the word "civilization" and covers all settled indigenous civilizations in Mexico and Central America prior to the Spanish conquest. The term is therefore quite broad, although all of these societies had comparable belief systems, architecture, culture, and cultivation systems, which evolved over centuries. To put it in perspective, Mesoamerica was as varied as Western Europe at the time of the Spanish conquest, and what occurred in the sixteenth century was not so much the discovery of a New World as the meeting of two previously separate branches of humanity. But let's start at the beginning. History prior to the conquest can be divided into four periods.

The Pre-Ceramic Period (6000–2500 BCE)

This period marks the beginning of agriculture, if not actual settlement on any significant scale. Seminomadic tribes used the kind of slash-and-burn agriculture that is not doing much for the Amazon and other forests these days: trees are cleared, crops are planted, and the people move on when the soil is exhausted, typically after three years. As the name suggests, evidence of the use of pottery only emerges right at the end of this period.

The Pre-Classic Period (2500 BCE–1 CE)

The Pre-Classic period saw small tribal states gradually (i.e. over centuries) emerging from a settled agrarian economy. Sophisticated pottery and weaving evolved alongside agricultural techniques, enabling people to form more permanent settlements. Eventually, the first large-scale Mesoamerican civilization, the Olmec (1500–400 BCE), began to develop, in the hot and humid jungles of the Gulf coast around what is now the state of Veracruz. Their most substantial city, at present-day La Venta, was at its peak in around 900 BCE and was abandoned by 400 BCE. Little is known about the Olmec but their influence on subsequent cultures is not in doubt. Their huge basalt sculptures of heads with rounded features, their hieroglyphs, calendar system, and extensive trading networks mean that they are sometimes called the *cultura madre,* or mother culture.

The Classic Period (1–1000 CE)

This period was dominated by two civilizations, the Maya, and that of Teotihuacán, but they were by no means the only ones.

Teotihuacán

The lack of a written history means that we also have little knowledge about the society based at the great city of Teotihuacán (even the name comes from the Aztec and means "the place where men became gods" in Nahuatl), a site thirty miles north of Mexico City, but the scale of the place is awe-inspiring even now, with the Pyramids of the Sun and Moon towering over the valley floor. At its peak in the fourth and fifth centuries CE, the city could have housed 125,000 souls—larger than any in Europe.

The Maya

The Maya were the other great civilization of the era. During the Classic period their influence spread across the jungles of northern Guatemala and Honduras and into present-day Chiapas (the site at Palenque is the best-preserved in Mexico from this time), but their power had faded by around 800 CE. Theirs was a theocratic society, based on independent city-states rather than a central authority (as was the pattern in central Mexico). Their scientific and artistic achievements, as well as their development of complex calendar, writing, and counting systems, mean that the Maya were once thought to have been peaceful, but it is now known that they were as keen on conquest and human sacrifice as any of their contemporaries.

Other Civilizations of the Classic Period

The Zapotec civilization (c. 1000 BCE–800 CE) also reached its high point early in this period. Its influence was never as widespread as that of the Maya, but it deserves a mention for its capital city at Monte Albán. Sitting astride a mountain spur above the city of Oaxaca, it is one of the most stunning archaeological sites in Mexico.

Another hugely impressive site from the period is El Tajín, in the jungles of Veracruz on the Gulf coast. However, apart from its origins in the Classic period, and the date of its rediscovery, 1785, little is known about the site. It is possibly a

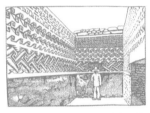

Huastec or Totonac city (both were powers in the region during that time), like Zempoala (the first indigenous city encountered by Cortes in 1519) further south, but unlike that one had been abandoned long before the conquest.

The Dark Ages

A gradual decline into a Mesoamerican equivalent of the Dark Ages occurred at the end of the Classic period, from around 750 CE onward. Deforestation and soil erosion played a crucial part, as agricultural resources were stretched to the breaking point by an ever-growing population. The net result was that barbarian tribes invaded from the north, cities were abandoned, and empires collapsed, although not entirely in some cases. The Maya, for example, reemerged in the north of the Yucatán peninsula in around 900 CE. Considerable archaeological remains can still be seen at prominent sites such as Chichen Itza, Uxmal, and Tulum.

The Post-Classic Period (1000–1520 CE)

While the Maya cities of the Yucatán were relatively peaceful during the Post-Classic period, it was a different story in central areas. Invasion from the north was the era's key threat, and essentially made war and conquest, always a feature of Mesoamerican culture, the *raison d'être* of successive societies. A series of barbarian, or "Chichimec" tribes arrived in the fertile central Mexican valley and attempted to establish their own society's dominance while also adopting many of the region's customs and religious systems. Most had only fleeting success, but two in particular stand out: the Toltec and, most impressive of all, the Aztec.

The Toltec

Originally one of the barbarian tribes, the militaristic Toltec dominated central and southern Mexico from around 1000–1200, and adapted the preexisting religion and culture of Teotihuacán to their own warlike tendencies. A cycle of war and sacrifice became the norm, both in response to the prevailing climate of violence, and also as the central element of Toltec ideology. Conquest yielded prisoners for human sacrifice, and increased sacrifice fueled society's appetite for war. The Toltec founded their capital at modern-day Tula, and their empire, the first genuine one of the Post-Classic period, spread far and their influence even wider. The Mayan city of Chichén Itzá in the  Yucatán, for example, a huge distance away even nowadays, is full of examples of Toltec art and architecture.

War and conquest continued after the fall of the Toltec, but for two hundred years or so it took place between smaller city-states and kingdoms. No single tribe was able to exert its dominance over central Mexico until the rise of the Aztec—the greatest empire of them all.

The Aztec

The wandering Mexica tribe founded their capital, Tenochtitlán, in 1345 on an island in the middle of Lake Texcoco, where, as had been prophesied, they had seen an eagle perched on a cactus devouring a snake. The city is now buried under the historical center of Mexico City (its central ceremonial pyramid, the Templo Mayor, was uncovered in 1978 and is now a museum) and the lake has long since been built over (save for a small network of canals in the southern suburb of Xochimilco) but the symbol endures as the central motif of Mexico's national flag. In the early fifteenth century, the Mexica made a series of alliances with local tribes around the shores of the lake, and together they became known as the Aztec, with the Mexica always the dominant force. Within a hundred years of these beginnings the Aztec empire stretched from coast to coast, and Tenochtitlán, with 200,000 inhabitants, was larger than any city in Europe at the time.

This rapid rise can be explained by the Aztec outlook on life, as reflected in their choice of tribal god, Huitzilopochtli. As god of war, he was already a significant deity in Toltec times, but he rose to dominate Aztec culture with every conquest. His unquenchable appetite for human flesh was reflected in his tribe's thirst for war. At this time societies in general were geared up for war as a matter of necessity and self-defense, but for the Aztec this tendency was also driven by religious fervor.

The priestly classes dominated Aztec society, as with every other society since Olmec times, but warriors were accorded an equal status. Senior state officials were the final component of the ruling elite, with urban artisans, merchants, and rural community leaders providing a middle layer to society. The vast majority of Aztecs enjoyed the same level of privilege as their European serf counterparts at the time: nil. They were either employed as servants, or worked the land to feed hungry armies and cities, and were only marginally better off than slaves taken in battle.

The empire functioned according to a system of tribute, under which goods flowed from both Aztec and conquered territories to the capital, Tenochtitlán. The Aztec implanted colonies in newly conquered territories, supported by permanent garrisons, and imposed Aztec religion and language. The system worked well, but it took an outsider to see the weakness behind its all-conquering self-image.

The Spanish Conquest

The story of how Hernan Cortés and 550 soldiers conquered this vast empire is an extraordinary one, involving prophecy, horses, firepower, diplomacy, guile, alliances, treachery, a fortuitous linguistic train (see Myths of the Conquest box, below), and much more besides. Cortés's unflinching determination (he burned his boats upon arrival) and his ability to form strategic alliances with enemies of the Aztec, such as the permanently-at-war Tlaxcalans, are the crucial factors. They are perhaps not the most romantic or dramatic, however, and many stories also look to Aztec mythology and superstition for an explanation. All good myths have an essential and often historical truth to them buried beneath the poetic license and imagery. In this case, it is that the Aztecs hesitated when they should not have; and that Cortés made alliances where he might not, in other circumstances, have been able to do so. In both instances a scapegoat has been found.

The Colonial Era

The conquest effectively continued during the early colonial period, with European diseases such as smallpox decimating a native population. In addition, no Spaniard ever came to New Spain, as it was known, to do manual labor, so Indians became even more like slaves than they had been under the feudal Aztec system. One empire replaced another as the Spanish built (or had built for them) hundreds of towns and monasteries, and thousands of churches.

Mass conversions by Franciscan monks took place in early colonial times, and the Church appeared to show genuine concern for the well-being of all. This wasn't to last. Landowners demanded cheap (i.e. forced) labor, and as the

MYTHS OF THE CONQUEST

Like the Toltec before them, the Aztec, and their emperor, Moctezuma, believed that Quetzalcoatl, a fair-skinned, bearded god who took the form of a Plumed Serpent, had been driven out of their capital, Tula, by his enemies and that he would return from the east and usher in a golden and peaceful age. When the fair-skinned, bearded Cortés landed in 1519, at around the date predicted for the god's return, he—and all the Spaniards in fact—seemed to fit the bill. One of Cortés's first acts was to ban human sacrifice in all the territory he conquered or allied himself with.

Poets have damned Moctezuma for not recognizing the Spaniards as invaders and historians have bemoaned his indecisiveness. But hindsight is a wonderful thing and this version of history does both Moctezuma and Cortés a disservice. The emperor could not have imagined that Cortés and his small band had come to conquer the Aztec empire—especially as Cortés kept his intentions hidden until he reached the capital, Tenochtitlán. Nor could he was comprehend, until too late, their greed for gold and their determination to get it.

Moctezuma was killed in June 1520, while a prisoner of the Spanish in the center of Tenochtitlán. According to the account of Bernal Díaz, one of Cortés's lieutenants, he was stoned by a crowd of his own subjects as he urged them to end their siege and let the Spaniards leave, something he evidently hoped, until the end, that they would do.

Crucial to Cortés's success was his ability to communicate with potential allies and enemies alike. Shortly after his first landing, he came across a Maya-speaking Spaniard, Jerónimo de Aguilar, who had been shipwrecked on the coast in 1513 and proved an invaluable asset in his first encounters. Inland, however, the dominant language was the Aztecs' Nahuatl, and Cortés would have struggled even more had he not been given a woman by a local chief who spoke both Maya and Nahuatl—Malintzin, or Doña Marina to the Spanish. She bore Cortés a son—who was effectively the first Mexican—and grew with every revisionist telling into the mythical figure of La Malinche, the woman who betrayed her people and their Mesoamerican paradise to the rapacious Spaniards.

Essentially, the problem was the cultural ocean between Spain and the Aztec empire. Where Mesoamerican war was religious in essence (the capturing of bodies to be sacrificed to appease a vengeful god), the Spaniards, seeking gold and glory, were willing to take the boldest risks with the minimum of scruples in order to enrich themselves and their reputations. But, to cut a long story very short, Cortés came, saw, and conquered, and there followed three hundred years of Spanish rule.

Church itself gradually became the colony's largest landowner, its perspective changed, and Indians were the casualties. An estimated indigenous population of 25 million at the time of conquest had been reduced by disease, persecution, and penury to less than half of the six million inhabitants of New Spain in 1800.

In the meantime, however, a new society began to take shape. Above the Indian and black slave underclass were an ever-increasing number of *mestizos*, people of mixed Indian and Spanish descent, and sitting proudly above these were an upper class of *criollos* (Creoles), people born in Mexico of Spanish descent. These became fabulously rich and, paradoxically, increasingly resentful of direct Spanish rule. They owned huge and highly profitable *haciendas* (large estates, either farms or ranches depending on the terrain) and mines, but these were designed principally to benefit the mother country.

This was a colony, after all, run for the enrichment of Spain by the monarch's representative in Mexico, the viceroy. No  trade other than with Spain was allowed, nor was any trade or agriculture that would compete with Spanish producers, and, probably crucially given

the Creoles' self-regard, no one born outside
Spain could hold high office in Mexico.
Independence eventually followed when Spain
entered a sharp period of decline in the late
eighteenth century.

Independence

Napoleon's occupation of the Iberian peninsula in
1808 was the catalyst. Ferdinand VII was deposed
and a power vacuum opened up in the distant
colonies. The earliest attempt to fill this with
something new is celebrated as a national holiday
in Mexico. Father Miguel Hidalgo y Costilla, a
Creole priest, gave the first cry of independence
from the steps of his church in Dolores on
September 16, 1810—"*Mexicanos ¡viva México!*"—
and, alongside army officer Ignacio Allende, was
soon at the head of an independence army
entering Mexico City. However, the following year
an absence of tactical ability saw it defeated, and
Allende and Hidalgo executed.

But the seeds had been sown, and the
independence movement gained new momentum
under the genuinely radical José María Morelos in
1813, before again being crushed in 1815. With
liberal reforms in Spain, though, the Creoles who
had fought against the insurgents were now eager
to break away from the colonial power before
these reforms could take root in Mexico.

Ex-royalists under Agustín de Iturbide and ex-insurgents under Vicente Guerrero then joined forces and in 1821 presented the *fait accompli* of Mexican independence to Spain, in the form of the Iguala Plan. Mexico was independent at last, the Creoles and the Church were still in charge, only more so, and a century that had started with the promise of freedom descended into calamity, confusion, and often outright farce.

Turmoil and Reform

The statistics give some idea of the chaos: in the forty years after 1821, Mexico went through fifty-six governments of one kind or another, including eleven under the utterly compelling (for all the wrong reasons) figure of General Santa Ana, and lost over half its national territory to the U.S.A. Texas seceded from Mexico in 1836 and joined the U.S.A. in 1845, while New Mexico, Nevada, Arizona, Colorado, and California were all signed over to the U.S.A. in 1848. Again, this was mostly attributable to Santa Ana, whose ability to bounce back from catastrophe and disgrace was perhaps his only genuinely impressive quality. Having lost two major wars against the U.S.A. and won one small one apiece against Spain and France, he eventually went into exile in Venezuela in 1855, minus his right leg, which had been blown off by a French cannon at Veracruz in 1838.

Civil War

But despite all the upheaval, little had changed:
the Church and the Creoles were still dominant
and the peasantry still put upon. Following Santa
Ana's exile, liberal attempts at even the mildest
reform provoked a reaction from the Church and
its conservative supporters. The most important
such effort was the Constitution of 1857, one of
the key moments in Mexican history. Drafted by
liberal leader and president Benito Juárez, a
Zapotec Indian and lawyer, it included
many points of contention, focusing
on the issues of Church and land
reform. The conservatives wanted no
change to the status quo, while the liberals
did. The Constitution guaranteed land
rights to dispossessed Indians and,
crucially, omitted to declare Mexico a
Catholic nation. State and Church were
separated, and the Church, constitutionally, had
no more political power.

The ensuing civil war was never in doubt, and
the country duly polarized into liberals who shot
priests, and conservatives who executed liberals.
The ten years of conflict had several different
phases. Four years of civil war were followed by
foreign intervention from Britain, Spain, and
France, which had occupied Veracruz in early
1862 over the nonpayment of bonds. The first two

eventually withdrew, but the French force stayed, apparently with a hidden plan. Sure enough, yet another strange episode in Mexican history soon followed: the rule of Archduke Maximilian, of the house of Habsburg, as emperor of Mexico.

A Mexican Emperor

The hapless Maximilian was invited to rule as emperor by the conservatives, at the behest of the French emperor Napoleon III, who wanted to ally Mexico with European powers as a bulwark against the "Anglo-Saxons" in the U.S.A. and elsewhere. At the time the U.S.A. was torn by its own civil war and could not enforce the Monroe Doctrine. By 1863 Napoleon's army had moved on to Mexico City.

Maximilian arrived in 1864 with no knowledge of Mexico, and immediately lost the support of conservatives when he proved to be a liberal at heart. In fact, the alternative constitution he proposed was at least as liberal as Juárez's. When French support also evaporated in 1866, as Napoleon III started worrying about his eastern border with Prussia, Maximilian was doomed. His few liberal supporters deserted him for the resurgent Juárez. He was defeated and executed by firing squad in June 1867, leaving a wife, Carlota, who went mad in exile, and a beautiful palace in Mexico City's Chapultepec Park.

From Reform to Dictatorship

Under Juárez, economic reconstruction began, but it was only after his death in 1872 that the pace began to pick up, under another liberal who quickly ditched his reformist background to rule as *de facto* dictator (he was reelected, but the elections were rigged) from 1876 to 1911. Porfirio Díaz oversaw massive growth in industry and infrastructure, although this was achieved mostly by selling these to foreign investors. Otherwise, the country, and certainly the countryside, took a step backward. Rich landowners became very rich, and peasants effectively became serfs. Censorship and internal repression were the order of the day, with corruption increasingly rife. Mexico looked set for another period of upheaval, especially as Díaz was growing old.

Revolution and Chaos

The Mexican Revolution began as a middle-class movement against Díaz's bias toward foreign investors. Francisco I. Madero, from one of the richest families in Coahuila but styling himself the "Apostle of Democracy," stood in the 1910 presidential election against Díaz (who won, as usual) and was imprisoned for his trouble. He managed to escape to Texas, where an opportunistic call to arms sparked uprisings across the country, with laborers and workers giving vent to their frustrations. In the north, the largest was in Chihuahua, under Pascual Orozco and former bandit Pancho Villa, while in the southern state of Morelos Indians rose up under Emiliano Zapata, but there were many other uprisings. These forced negotiations between the rebels and the soon-to-be ex-government, and by October 1911 Díaz was in exile and Madero was president, following free elections. But this being Mexico, it was impossible to satisfy every faction, and it all gradually unraveled. Zapata continued his insurrection in the south, the U.S.A. abandoned Madero, and various factions plotted bloodily against one another.

By early 1913, army general Victoriano Huerta was in power, Madero had been assassinated, and the two sides of the struggle had taken shape. Ranged against the old oligarchs of the capital, represented by Huerta, was an alliance of powerful northern landowners and industrialists led by Álvaro Obregón and Venustiano Carranza, the governors of Sonora and Coahuila respectively. Essentially, each faction wanted the same thing: power. Villa and Zapata were allied with the northerners but can be excused from this generalization—they at least fought for revolutionary aims, Villa's personal vanity (he sometimes went into battle with an American film crew) notwithstanding. Zapata's motto, "*Tierra y Libertad*" ("Land and Freedom"), has been resurrected by modern-day Zapatistas (*plus ça change!*). The northern faction had triumphed by the end of 1914 and installed Carranza as president, but this in no way signaled the end of the bloodshed.

On the contrary, the country took a turn for the worse, descending into anarchy as local and regional factions made and broke alliances with each other. On a national level, Villa, Zapata, and other "conventionalists" (who had agreed on radical land redistribution at the 1914 Aguascalientes Convention) took up arms again when it became clear that this "Constitutionalist" government was substantially similar to the last. By the end of 1915, however, Villa had been pushed back to Chihuahua and Zapata to Morelos, and the revolutionary part of the Revolution was over, even if the horrendous violence continued: around 10 to 12 percent of the entire population of Mexico was killed between 1910 and 1920.

Modern Mexico Emerges

Rebuilding a modern state was to prove difficult. The Revolution had ended through exhaustion on all sides rather than resolution, although the Constitution of 1917 contained most of the insurgents' demands and is still in effect. The trouble was in implementing them. Carranza had no intention of doing so, but his successors, prominent among them Plutarco Elías Calles, made significant progress despite their obvious corruption. Barring a minor civil war between anticlericals and Church supporters, the country was at peace by 1934.

As if by a miracle, Mexico had redefined itself as a thriving, artistic republic, and a haven for political exiles from across the world, celebrating itself in vast murals by artists like Diego Rivera, David Alfaro Siqueiros, and José Clemente Orozco. These depicted Mexico as an ancient indigenous power, interrupted on its course by the arrival of Spaniards, but now back on the right path. Given its painful colonial and more recent history, this new mythology was exactly what Mexico needed.

The resurgent country also got the president it deserved when the aptly named Lázaro Cárdenas was elected in 1934. His influence on Mexico cannot be overstated. Having forced Calles and his cronies into exile in 1936, he set out actually to achieve some of the Constitution's paper promises. He redistributed land on a massive scale and set up trade unions and workers' organizations, while also (and this is the cunning part) building them into the structure of the PRN, or Party of National Revolution (the broad party, founded in 1928, that later became the PRI, or Party of Institutional Revolution, which ruled Mexico until the year 2000). This crucial network had the government's ear, but it also had theirs.

Perhaps the most significant move of his presidency, certainly in economic terms, came in 1938 when he nationalized the many foreign oil companies operating in Mexico. It was nothing if not good timing. The outbreak of the Second World War led to a thirst for oil in countries that might have organized a damaging boycott (i.e., the U.S.A.), and Mexico was one of the few countries to benefit from six years of global chaos.

Stability and Growth

For thirty or more years Mexico's economy grew, on a foundation of oil production, and it seemed that the PRI could do little wrong. Its presidents served out their six-year terms in peace without seeking reelection and without losing much public support. Mexico became a unique blend of intensive capitalist development and revolutionary nationalism under the PRI. Under Miguel Alemán's presidency (1946–52), the rate of industrialization, and its conjoined twin, urbanization, began to accelerate.

MEXICAN OIL

Twentieth-century Mexico has been built to a significant extent on oil. In 2002 it produced 3.5 million barrels of oil per day, making it the world's fifth-largest producer. Although it has nothing like the oil reserves of Saudi Arabia and Kuwait, and its near neighbor Venezuela, they are still vast, and current production rates are projected to be sustainable for up to fifty years.

Commercial production of crude oil began in 1901 on the Gulf coast, and peaked in 1921, when Mexico produced a quarter of the world's oil. This tailed off, however, with the emergence of Venezuela as an oil producer and long disputes with foreign oil companies, which led to the nationalization in 1938 and the creation of Pemex (Petroleos Mexicanos), the state oil company. New oil fields were periodically discovered, but demand eventually caught up with output and by 1957 Mexico was a net importer of oil.

This lasted until the early 1970s, when huge oil reserves were discovered in Chiapas and again on the Gulf coast. The global energy crisis of 1973 led to gigantic export earnings for Mexico once again. These were plowed back into the country's oil production infrastructure (and often into officials' very deep pockets), a move that ensured Mexico continued to produce oil on a large scale but did nothing for the country's national debt as oil prices fell again.

The policy of reinvestment continues, however, with Mexico constantly adding to its own oil-refining capacity, allowing it greater profit margins at export relative to crude oil. That is the theory, but another obstacle to profit has been endemic corruption, which looks to have peaked in the late 1980s. A systematic cleanup of the huge Pemex beast has led to greater profitability since the early 1990s, and even foreign investment in oil-related industries, unthinkable just fifteen years ago. Successive governments have insisted that this is not privatization on the sly, but it has increasingly looked that way.

Urbanization and Industrialization

Manufacturing grew rapidly from the 1940s onward on the back of the oil industry, especially in Mexico City (and the Federal District), Puebla, Guadalajara, Monterrey, and eleven other cities close to the U.S. border. Urbanization was the inevitable by-product. Initially, growth centered on vehicle, chemical, and machinery manufacture. Areas of subsequent industrial development included textiles and food

processing, as well as heavy industries such as metal fabrication, cement, and paper mills. Located in industrial belts around cities, these remain magnets that attract migrants from poor rural areas.

Massive, often unplanned neighborhoods sprang up to house these workers. Many of them are now well-established districts, well within city limits, if still rather grim to live in, but the poorest and most desperate remain ever-growing shanty-towns. A thousand people a day are said to flock to Mexico City alone, and plenty more move to the twelve *maquiladora* (assembly plant) towns along or near the U.S. border, which still attract by far the most foreign investment per head of population in the country.

So, industry took the place of agriculture as Mexico's main economic motor, but otherwise the PRI both steered the ship and effectively was the ship. However, apart from a brief swerve to the left in the late 1950s and early 1960s, this vessel was moving steadily to the right, and the balancing act of being both pro-business and pro-workers became nigh-on impossible to manage.

Protest and Dissent: 1968 in Mexico

In 1968 it could all have unraveled. As in many other countries worldwide, the student left protested in large numbers. These protests usually followed accepted conventions, by which the students were allowed to make their point, in this case a show of support for Fidel Castro's Cuba, as long as they mostly "behaved." But in a Mexico City that was about to show itself off to the world by hosting the Olympic Games, this sort of dissent suddenly could not be tolerated, and the situation quickly came to a head. Initial demonstrations in August and September were put down far more violently than before, which only added to the tension. On October 2, hundreds of students were massacred in the center of Mexico City by security forces, who opened fire without warning on an unarmed crowd. Mexico found itself on the receiving end of worldwide condemnation, and began to question the image it had of itself: was it really the kind of country that slaughtered its own young people?

Support was peeling off from both ends of the PRI's previously broad church: to guerrilla movements on the left and to the rival party, PAN (Party of National Action, that of the current president, Vicente Fox), on the right. Brutal repression accounted for the former, while a (some might say cynical) blend of populist measures and socialist rhetoric kept the bulk of the PRI's support in place. But all was not well within the PRI, and nowhere was this more obvious than in their handling of the economy.

The Economy Stutters

The 1970s saw budget deficits and inflation grow. Alongside this, corruption and graft grew from a covert but tolerated feature of political life into something far more brazen, and the wheels began to loosen under the PRI chariot, although they took another quarter century to come off. The peso was devalued in 1976, and the economy appeared to stabilize under an IMF-imposed austerity program. However, those affected most severely were poorer Mexicans, employed or not, as wages were effectively halved and jobs became scarcer.

A massive windfall, in the form of the discovery of huge new oil reserves in the late 1970s, failed to rescue the country from further economic strife. The PRI's corporate state, with its culture of patronage and favors, somehow absorbed the billions of dollars, when they could have corrected the country's balance of payments and wiped out its national debt. Instead, Mexico defaulted on its foreign debt in 1982, and plunged into a new round of austerity measures.

Austerity made the PRI's balancing act harder. It could not afford to remain the deeply flawed "philanthropic ogre" identified by Octavio Paz in his 1978 essay of the same name on Mexican government. With a huge debt to service, philanthropy was out of the question, and the ogre's usual heavy-handed repression could no longer silence a large and vocal opposition. Instead, scapegoats were chosen from among the greediest of party functionaries and prosecuted. This strategy might have worked for a time had Mexico City and the west of the country not been hit by a huge earthquake in 1985. Thousands of the country's poorest people lost their lives, and hundreds of thousands their homes. The government's response was completely inadequate, fueling massive public anger.

Mexico and the Free Market

The PRI finally attempted to change. Carlos Salinas de Gortari became president in 1988 after the first election in which an opposition candidate (Cuauhtémoc Cárdenas, son of Lázaro, officially won 32 percent of the vote and unofficially a good deal more) appeared to have a chance of winning. Salinas privatized huge sections of the public sector in an effort to liberalize the economy and thus stimulate growth and reduce debt. The pieces that remained, such as the state oil company Pemex, also fell under greater scrutiny. He also signed a debt-relief arrangement underwritten by the U.S. Treasury that was to pave the way for the North American Free Trade Area, or NAFTA, which covered the whole of the North American continent. This came into being in 1994, and was perhaps the most fundamental change in Mexico since the Revolution, launching the country into a genuinely free market that had little time for the PRI's traditional commitment to protectionism.

The Zapatista Uprising

Throughout Mexican history, attempts to force through massive change have met with an equal level of reaction. The change has usually been broadly liberal and the reaction conservative, but this time the reaction came from the left, specifically the rural indigenous poor of Chiapas, the country's southernmost state. The Zapatista Army of National Liberation, or ELZN, inspired by Emiliano Zapata and led by the pipe-smoking, balaclava-wearing Subcomandante Marcos, seized the town of San Cristóbal de las Casas and demanded redistribution of land and other resources and the repeal of NAFTA. The army reacted with predictable brutality, and forced the Zapatistas back into the jungles, but its repressive tactics did Mexico's image abroad no favors, the government quickly entered negotiations, and a cease-fire was achieved in 1995. But that was only a beginning. The 1994 presidential election was contested and won, apparently honestly, by the PRI candidate, Ernesto Zedillo, amid increasing violence across the country.

The rise of the drug cartels explains some of the mayhem, but another uprising in Chiapas and the emergence of another guerrilla movement in neighboring Guerrero were clear symptoms of increasing polarization. Military brutality escalated into paramilitary massacres, which in turn provoked more international condemnation. The government backed off, and a kind of standoff has been in effect ever since, although negotiations have once again been entered into.

Mexico after the PRI

The year 2000 saw Vicente Fox, the opposition
PAN candidate, elected as president. After a quarter
century of gradual erosion, the PRI monopoly was
finally broken. The transition has been remarkably
peaceful. This is mostly because the presidency was
only the last of many institutions where the PRI's
power had waned. The PRI still wields significant
influence, however, and change has been slower
than promised. The sluggish pace of fiscal reform
has caused frustration in the wider business world,
while anticorruption measures have yet to clear out
the bureaucracy. But reform is under way, and
Fox's commitment to education and resolving the
Zapatista issue once and for all (and nonviolently)
has maintained his popularity, despite public
misgivings over new taxes such as VAT on food—
and continuing, overwhelming poverty.

MEXICAN GOVERNMENT TODAY

Mexico's Federal Republican structure is similar to
that of the U.S.A. It has a presidential system, with
a constitutionally strong Congress, which is
divided into two chambers, the 128-seat Senate,
which has elections every six years, and the
Chamber of Deputies, a 500-member body with
three-year terms. State governors are elected for
six-year terms, and state assemblies have the

power to levy statewide taxes. The federal legal system also gives significant autonomy to individual state courts, although Mexico also has a Supreme Court.

The president himself is also elected for a fixed six-year term. The "no reelection" clause in the Constitution of 1917 remains a counterweight to the excesses that can occur when a president is reelected—as happened during the Porfiriato dictatorship.

The current president, Vicente Fox, heads a minority government, and the right-of center Party of National Action (PAN). The old Party of Institutional Revolution (PRI), for seventy years the only party in government, heads the opposition and is still a massive force in Mexican politics. It has the largest share of the Senate (sixty seats compared to PAN's forty-eight) and the Chamber of Deputies, with 222 seats, compared to PAN's 151. The other main party is the Party of Democratic Revolution (PRD), which has sixteen senators and ninety-five deputies. A significant minority party is the Green Party (PVEM), which has five senators and seventeen deputies.

chapter two

VALUES &
ATTITUDES

The extremes of poverty and wealth in Mexico
make it difficult to generalize about Mexicans
without leaving at least some people out. But one
thing that can safely be said is that it is a Catholic
country, and devoutly so. Many common
values hold sway and can be readily
identified. This Catholicism has its own
uniquely Mexican flavor, with roots in
missionary pragmatism, whereby
Christian festivals were blended with
old indigenous rituals for ease of
consumption by the people. Individuals
chose conversion and salvation as an
obvious line of least resistance, and the
result is that, nearly five hundred years after the
Spanish conquest, pre-Columbian beliefs are alive
and well. For most of the country, these have been
dressed up in Catholic clothes, but for a large
minority in around sixty indigenous
communities, they are remarkably intact.

And it is not just in spiritual matters that
Mexico's unique history has helped forge a

national identity. Their often spectacularly violent history has given Mexicans a familiarity with death and a fatalistic outlook that is beyond the Western experience, even allowing for its two World Wars. The country's defining festival is the Day of the Dead (see Chapter 3, Customs and Traditions). The name itself says a great deal.

Some visitors to Mexico are tempted to remark how *different* it is from the U.S.A, with which it shares a long land border, or indeed anywhere else. While the American and Western model has been successfully exported around the globe, this is not something that Mexico seeks to emulate. You will find parts of the country, some very close to the U.S. border, where the outlook on life is as different from that of the West as anywhere on the planet. Mexico is proudly, vibrantly, and unashamedly itself. And for all its considerable diversity, you will encounter a warm and welcoming person beneath many a gruff exterior, if you bring an open mind.

THE FAMILY

It is difficult to describe a typical Mexican family. In the richest families children may be brought up by nannies and rarely seen by parents, while in the poorest economic necessity often sees families broken up as various members move off to an uncertain future in a distant town, or even in that huge country to the north. Nevertheless, the family remains the paramount institution in Mexico, reinforced by factors such as Catholicism and financial pressure.

The extended family gathers regularly to celebrate birthdays, saints' days, public holidays, births, and marriages, and for funerals. Family members like to live close to each other, although the modern world long ago encroached upon traditional Mexican family structures, and migration in search of work, or to study, is a fact of life. A more recent development is the increase in the number of women pursuing careers or

simply needing to work in order to feed the family, and in these cases grandparents are often relied upon to mind the children. This has created a newer phenomenon in which it is not just single young people who move to the cities (and send money back home), but three generations of one family, who will all depend on the middle generation's earnings.

For the Mexican who does move away from home, the concept of family is so ingrained that it can be a struggle to get used to life without the support of that strong network—although, once the break has been made, returning to the intrusions of an oversupportive family can also be a problem. Overall, though, Mexicans find it hard not to see the more Western tradition of moving away from home at the age of eighteen and never returning as a sure sign of a family in crisis.

Children are doted on, and are involved in and shown off at all manner of social gatherings at all times of the day or night. It's not unusual to see children dropped off at the school gates looking bleary-eyed, their hair being tamed by their mothers with water and lemon juice.

The result of this zealous nurturing is often bipolar. On the one hand, Mexican children generally grow up to be confident individuals. On the other, they often grow used to having things done for them, and to being the center of attention at all times.

Even now, many young people don't leave home until they are married. This is not just for reasons of economy: most of their needs are catered to in the bosom of their family (meals, washing, etc.) and they are left with a lot of freedom to socialize. Parents rarely encourage offspring to leave home or fend for themselves, although in recent years the young have started to contribute toward living costs. Few are required to help around the house (especially the men).

In Mexican society, the elderly are well-respected and generally looked after within the family unit, with three or four generations living together under the same roof not unusual. Again, this is only partly for economic reasons.

Family breakdown is often apparent in the poorer parts of big cities, where there is not only a high incidence of single mothers, but a lot of "street children," which shocks many visitors.

FRIENDS AND ACQUAINTANCES

A Mexican has many acquaintances and few friends. This is probably true of many other people, but Mexicans are perhaps more honest, and the boundaries are more clearly delineated—it is difficult to make friends, certainly, and you are unlikely to be led into believing a relationship on a superficial level is anything other than that. This is not to say that Mexicans are unfriendly (on the contrary, they are very welcoming), just that long-lasting friendships tend to be made at an early age, at primary school level, where the friend in question almost becomes part of the family (it always comes back to the family!). In adulthood, these close-knit groups of friends are hard to break into. People tend to socialize with their old friends, siblings, cousins, and brothers/sisters-in-law, which leaves little time for new friendships. When these are made, it is usually within the same social class, often through the workplace, though most relationships here never go beyond the realms of "acquaintance."

For foreigners trying to make friends, some common ground, a shared interest, or even simply a profession in common, will help. Social boundaries will be less restrictive for you—as a foreigner you don't belong to a particular class.

Insult or Affection?

Being called "*gordo*" (fatty), "*flaco*" (skinny), or even "*negro*" (blackie) may or may not be meant as an insult, depending on how well you are known to the person doing the name-calling. If that person is a total stranger, it's safe to assume that he or she is trying to offend you. In Mexico, however, such personal remarks are signs of affection between close friends. A person's most obvious features, flattering or not, are often worked into their nickname in a way that might surprise those used to superficial social "niceties."

PRIDE, HONOR, AND *MACHISMO*

In the West, *machismo* has become a byword for unreconstructed misogyny, and is a word that is often used in conjunction with Mexican men. However, in Mexico the women of the family are respected, even revered. This is one of many

Mexican paradoxes. A man shouting pleasant *piropos*, or "compliments" ("*guapa*," or "gorgeous," being a standard one), at a girl in the street would be mortified if he felt he was causing offense. There is nothing malicious about it, and certainly no offense is intended. Sometimes, however, less pleasant things are shouted in the streets.

Of course, reverence and misogyny are not mutually exclusive—a man can place a woman on a pedestal while also considering her unsuited to certain occupations (or occupations in general). Mexican men, by Western standards, are sexist, but that does not make them slavering brutes, or Mexican women meek and cowering. The reality is that, if the family is paramount in Mexico, then women are in charge—and mothers are the *patronas* (bosses), as we shall see in Chapter 5. Mexico is a thoroughly matriarchal society, and *machismo* is simply the flip side of the same coin. It could be argued that such attitudes are an obstacle on the road to genuine equality, but then this is not a book on gender politics.

It follows from this (somewhat perversely, but it does) that the worst insults in Mexico are directed at a man's mother. This has to do with respect for women among the country's men, as well as with pride in general, which is embodied in various other things a man cherishes: his family, his country, his soccer team. To insult them is to cause personal offense, unless it is in jest (and jest is only acceptable with time and friendship), and insults a man's honor. Fights are not unusual in these circumstances, especially if alcohol has been added to the mix. Women are far more sensible about these things. Another aspect of pride is that Mexicans will rarely say "I don't know," and will *always* give an answer—even a taxi driver who has no clue where he is going.

Shamed!

A little illustration of *machismo*, shame, and criminality . . . One evening in Mexico City, two men attempted to snatch a woman's purse, whereupon she remonstrated loudly with them. She asked them, "How would you feel if this happened to your mother or sister?" They apologized profusely, and left her alone. She was lucky, though—it is probably best not to try this one yourself.

BEATING THE SYSTEM

The concept of "society" is not strong in urban Mexico. Mexicans are intensely patriotic and proud of their country, but not necessarily full of civic pride in the institutions that run it—another Mexican parado, perhaps. Solidarity and community are not common currency—it is more about "Me versus Society." This attitude applies to dealings with officialdom and state agencies (the taxman and the police are two examples), and stems from the fact that long-standing corruption and inefficiency has robbed them of much of their legitimacy in the eyes of the people. Reversing this trend and thus instilling belief in the apparatus of state has been the central aim of Vicente Fox and his PAN party, but it has been tough going after decades of official inertia and complacency.

In smaller towns, and certainly in villages, a sense of community still prevails. In rural states such as Chiapas, Oaxaca, and Morelos whole political movements are rooted in a sense of solidarity and community, but these are protest movements and have only emerged in reaction to a remote central government. In the larger cities, people feel responsible to family and friends (in that order), but do not look far beyond that.

RESPECT FOR TRADITION

Tradition, whether it be Maya, Huichol, or Catholic, is still highly respected and observed across the country, especially in more rural areas such as the Yucatán peninsula (Maya), Oaxaca (Zapotec), Jalisco (Huicholes) and Chihuahua (Tarahumaras), to name but four of the indigenous language/cultural groups. In these areas, people still speak in the "old" language, eat "old" food, and celebrate the traditional festivals—it sometimes seems as if the Spanish never came. But overall, Catholicism's impact on the country was profound, and its institutions and traditions are hugely influential today: religious observance, whether out of piety or habit, remains strong (see Chapter 3 for more on this).

Unsurprisingly, young people's attitudes to traditions of any kind, especially the more "antiquated," are less enthusiastic, but they tend to mellow with age and remain in favor of any celebrations that involve a good party.

TOLERANCE AND PREJUDICES

In a country that, since independence, has seen it all ("it" mostly being epic levels of violence and civil war—essentially the prejudices held by some against the prejudices of others), a surprising degree of tolerance prevails. As the PRI's grip on the country's political and social life has loosened, Mexico has become a freer society. Political debate is up, censorship is down (both political and "moral"—sex is prominent on TV, in advertising, and on the newsstands, while graphic photographic accounts of the latest drug cartel murder are a staple of the weekly supplements), but Catholic conservatism still shapes many people's view of life.

Under Spanish rule, racial separation was enshrined in the class structure, with Spanish-born rulers right at the top of the pile, *criollos* (Creoles, born in New Spain of Spanish descent) forming an upper class, *mestizos* (literally, "mixtures" of Spanish and indigenous blood) in the middle, and indigenous people and black slaves at the bottom. After the Revolution, it became *de rigueur* for the country's artistic and political elite to claim indigenous heritage, but the reality remains that the whiter you are, the better-off you are likely to be, and in that sense people are still assessed on their skin color—how "Indian" you look will affect, if nothing else, how wealthy you are assumed to be (although a significant number of *mestizos* hold senior posts in the world of politics). Whether this counts as racism is debatable, as it describes economic reality, but making assumptions based on skin color is one of the less endearing Mexican traits. Like fair-haired foreigners, black people are likely to be stared at—usually only out of curiosity. This is mostly because there are not many black people in Mexico—but be aware that in smaller towns, "small-town" mentalities may well prevail.

Similar advice applies to gay and lesbian visitors. Mexico City has a large and lively gay community, but it has become large and lively mostly due to prejudice driving openly gay individuals away from smaller communities.

LIVING FOR THE MOMENT

In economic terms, prudence is seen as a bit misplaced in Mexico. People generally don't save their money, as experience has taught them the pointlessness of it. In a culture where devaluation (like the extended crises in the 1980s and in 1994) can overnight wipe out your life savings, or at least reduce them to next to nothing, this is understandable. But living for the moment is more than just an economic calculation, and goes back a lot further than the IMF. Fatalism runs deep in the Mexican character, and informs how many people's decisions are made. A natural exuberance within the Mexican character emerges *in extremis*, when worry and stress would be expected, and comes from the "certain" knowledge that it cannot last forever.

In terms of work, people work to live—or just survive in many cases—and don't understand the philosophy of living to work. Mexicans do put in long hours, and seek professional fulfillment, but the difference is that they seldom take their work home, and they prefer to entrust their personal happiness to family and friends.

MANNERS

Good manners are of great significance to the Mexicans, although, once you get to know them, formality and diffidence quickly give way to a friendly familiarity. It is very important to know how to address people on first meeting them (see Chapter 8). Familiarity may take a while, so when in doubt always err on the side of good manners. As in many other countries, the older generation in Mexico is more formal, and a certain respectful distance should be maintained.

Once you have made friends, social niceties are dispensed with. "Please" and "thank you" are unnecessary among friends and family, although the use of diminutives (—*ito*, —*ita*) is a common politeness. Mexicans can be very direct. You will be told if you are not looking your best (but you will also be told if you are, which is agreeable).

CLASS SYSTEMS: THE GREAT DIVIDE
Mexico City versus the Provinces
Mexico's rapid industrialization has left many people behind, although this is not to say that some don't remain "behind" out of defiant choice. In many rural areas, for example, indigenous communities have managed to maintain a traditional way of life in the face of growing homogenization in Mexico and the world at large.

As in many countries, a certain friction exists between the dominant capital city and everywhere else. *Chilangos*, as the residents of the Distrito Federal are known, are considered to be snobbish pseudosophisticates who look down their noses at the rest of Mexico. This is harsh but fair, because they do—wondering why anyone should even doubt that the capital is *the* place to be. It is a slightly patronizing point of view, but it is also true that Mexico City is the most exciting city in the country.

Many people do not, however, and the rural poor especially are not impressed with the urban-oriented view of the nation and of government—the cities grow "because they must"—while they are left to drift further away from mainstream society.

This is (somewhat simplistically) the motivation behind the Zapatista movement of the last ten years. It is essentially a campaign for social justice: its guerrilla tag comes from its tactics of melting into the landscape after making its point, and has rather less to do with the kind of "terror" more normally associated with guerrillas. That usually comes from the paramilitaries sent to crush them—a sledgehammer to the Zapatista nut. The protests that effectively sank the World Trade talks in Cancún in August 2003 were along similar lines.

Class

Attitudes to class have been touched upon in the section on prejudices above, but there are sharp social divisions within Mexico (40 percent of Mexicans live below the poverty line). It is only really in urban areas that you find a significant middle class, and a working, significant-wage-

earning class, between the richest and the poorest sections of society. In rural areas you are generally either one of the very few rich people or among the

millions of poor. Over the past fifty years, the rich have got richer and the poor poorer. Among the latter there is an unwillingness to change, and an acceptance of the status quo, and of their "place in society." Many young idealists go to Mexico to help the poor, and are baffled by their conservatism.

PROTEST AND DISSENT

Demonstrations and strikes occur frequently all across Mexico, although given the conditions many people live in there is far less protest and dissent than one would have imagined. There is a kind of stoic acceptance of conditions and situations. Thus, although people take part in huge demonstrations, and often bring the traffic in central Mexico City and other cities to a halt, this is mainly to express their grievances rather than in anticipation of any positive change. In Oaxaca state, for example, many teachers go on strike over pay and conditions most Fridays, even though subsequently nothing much happens.

MEXICO AND THE U.S.A.

Mexico's relationship with its northern neighbor has at times been fraught with tension. The U.S.A.'s influence on Mexican domestic politics has been felt well beyond the two wars they fought in the nineteenth century. U.S. support or lack thereof could make or break a pretender to the presidency, and the momentum of the Revolution was always with those who were supported by the U.S.A. and Woodrow Wilson.

After the Revolution, Mexico attempted to rid itself of foreign (i.e., U.S.) ownership of its utilities with a nationalization program (especially of the oil and mining industries). But the ensuing boycott did not prevent U.S. investment in other industries, as the entire border zone, with its U.S.-owned factories, demonstrates. As we have seen, NAFTA opened up most Mexican industries to U.S. and Canadian capital and ownership, but its impact is still being assessed. Mexico seems no less Mexican for NAFTA, although what benefit the majority of Mexicans will derive from it is unclear.

In terms of widely held attitudes, there is no love lost between the two countries. Mexicans are fiercely proud and protective of their own culture, especially in the face of a perceived (and probably real in many cases) insistence on the part of Americans in exporting theirs, be it in terms of how to do business or how to eat and relax. It has been described on a macro level as a master–servant relationship, and given the number of Mexicans working for U.S. companies in Mexico, this is not a bad assessment.

Individually, though, a warmer welcome awaits any visitor who shows some respect for and understanding of the country.

IMMIGRATION/EMIGRATION

There is a huge Mexican population in the U.S.A.—some eight million Mexican-born people live there officially, with millions more undocumented and virtually unacknowledged doing the menial jobs that keep the wheels running beneath American society and sending their (very) hard-earned cash home. Seasonal agricultural workers toil in the fields and orange groves of California and other border states, keeping food prices down in the U.S.A.

The huge fences along the U.S. border are actually secondary barriers to the primary ones on Mexico's southern border. Mexico is continually trying to keep Central Americans out (stricter border controls were written into the NAFTA accords), and the fences in Chiapas, Campeche, and Quintana Roo match those on the northern border. In addition, there are road blocks, police checkpoints throughout the three regions, and people in these areas are required to have their identity papers with them at all times.

ATTITUDES TO FOREIGNERS

Most Mexicans have a genuine inquisitiveness about foreigners, and their interest is not hostile, but may seem intrusive. They may stare, but it's only curiosity. They want to find out about you, and like to talk—above all to practice their English. They will ask you about your family, friends, money, and more intimate matters—if you are over 35 and have no children, for example, they may frown on you.

It is unlikely, unless you're well off the beaten track, that you will be the first foreigner they have ever seen—so don't feel too special!

chapter three

CUSTOMS & TRADITIONS

As we have seen, Mexican Catholicism is a product of the collision between the indigenous Mesoamerican belief-system and the religious zeal of the Spanish conquering force. Catholicism's association with Mexico began the day Cortés made his first landing on Cozumel Island, off the Yucatán peninsula, when an indigenous ceremony involving ritual sacrifice was broken up and a Mass said. Conquest had the blessing of both the king of Spain and the Pope, and though religious zeal may have been ousted by thoughts of treasure in the *conquistadores'* minds, conversion was nevertheless the secondary aim of conquest and its main justification.

FESTIVALS AND HOLIDAYS

As in other Latin American countries, and indeed Spain, *fiestas* feature prominently in Mexican culture. They are also taken very seriously, both by academics analyzing them for clues as to the Mexican national identity and by the participants themselves, who enter into the spirit of the *fiesta*, whatever the occasion, body and soul. But no matter how it may look to an outsider, any Mexican will tell you that a *fiesta* is more than simply a big party. Ordinary Mexicans look for a release from their often harsh daily existence in the sense of camaraderie and social cohesion that a *fiesta* provides and that is often lacking from day to day. Every community, be it a city neighborhood or a rural village, has its own patron saint, who is honored with an annual festival. These follow the rituals of the Catholic Church to some degree, though in more indigenous communities many owe more to pre-Columbian traditions than to Rome's influence. Neither does the hedonism of many such festivals have much to do with religion.

Mexico also has a whole range of regional and national festivals and holidays, some of them on a spectacular scale, and many going to the core of what it is to be Mexican.

THE FESTIVAL CALENDAR
January
• **The New Year** is celebrated by a midnight mass of thanksgiving for blessings bestowed over the previous year, followed by a public holiday on January 1.

• **Epiphany** (January 6). Children may open presents from the Three Kings, and eat a cake, the *rosca de reyes*, in which a small image of the baby Jesus is hidden.

February

• **Constitution Day** (February 5) is the second public holiday of the year, after New Year's Day.
• **Flag Day** (February 24) is a public holiday, and children parade and salute the national flag. Mayan handicrafts are on display at a major fair in Mérida in the Yucatán throughout February.
• **Carnaval** (or Carnival), a nine-day blowout before the privations of Lent, usually begins in late February or early March, depending on how late Easter falls. A major, colorful event across the country, it bears comparison with famous carnivals across the world. This is especially true of the festivities in Veracruz on the Gulf coast; Mazatlán in Sinaloa and Mérida in Yucatán also party on a grand scale. Parades, fireworks, and concerts are typical of Carnaval, but the soundtrack is the key: *samba*, *salsa*, and *marimba* rhythms fill the air, and people dance and dance.

March/April

• **Benito Juárez's birthday** (March 21) is celebrated as a public holiday.

• *Semana Santa*, Easter week, is taken as a vacation by most Mexicans (Easter Thursday and Friday are public holidays), with the more secular middle classes visiting the coast before the rainy season begins. It is more than just the country's biggest holiday, however—it remains a deeply religious festival. Processions take place during the day, with Good Friday the culmination. Passion plays are performed all over the country, but are especially worth seeing in smaller towns throughout Oaxaca state.

• *Feria de San Marcos*, a three-week affair, is held in San Marcos, in Aguascalientes state. It includes a large parade on April 25, St. Mark's Day. Typical of the festival are concerts, cockfights, bullfights, and *charreadas* (Mexican-style rodeo—see Chapter 6), with plenty of drinking, eating, and dancing thrown in for good measure.

May

• **Labor Day** (May 1). As in many other countries, trade unions march, politicians give speeches, and ordinary people mostly ignore them.

• *Cinco de Mayo*, or the Battle of Puebla (May 5), is a key date in the Mexican calendar. This national holiday is celebrated by Mexicans the world over. The focus of attention: on that day in

1862, Mexico defeated an invading French army at Puebla, on the road from Veracruz to the capital.

• **Mother's Day** (May 10). The importance of this holiday in a matriarchal society such as Mexico should not be underestimated and many offices award all the mothers working there an (unofficial) half day's holiday.

• **St. Isidore's Day** (May 15), when animals and agricultural tools are blessed, is likewise an important date in rural communities.

May/June

• **Corpus Christi** (celebrating the Real Presence of Christ in the Eucharist) falls on the first Thursday after Trinity Sunday. Church services and processions take place all over the country. Papantla, in Veracruz state, offers something different. Huastecan *voladores* (flyers), in a display dating from pre-Columbian times, climb a pole in groups of five. The ritual invokes fertility and honors the sun. The first four leap backward off a platform at the top, each attached to the pole by a rope, while the fifth performs a dance and plays drums and a whistle. As the rope unravels, each *volador* circles the pole thirteen times, to a total of fifty-two, which symbolize the fifty-two-year cycle of the Mesoamerican calendar.

• **Navy Day** (June 1) is an official holiday, with port towns organizing events to honor the navy.

July
• **Guelaguetza festival**, on the first two Mondays after July 16, takes place in Oaxaca state. It celebrates indigenous dances, such as the Zapotec feather dance, a symbolic reenactment of the Spanish conquest of Mexico.

September
• **Independence Day** (September 16) is a national holiday. Fireworks and music fill the air on the evening before. This is followed by a typically Mexican flourish as the president repeats Father Miguel Hidalgo's 1810 cry to arms, "El Grito" ("*Mexicanos, ¡viva México!*"), from the balcony of the Palacio Nacional in Mexico City center. Parades celebrating the independence heroes take place across the country on the following day.

October
• ***Descubrimiento de América*** (Discovery of America Day, October 12) has now become more a celebration of pre-Columbian Mexicans.
• ***Festival Internacional Cervantino,*** in October, is one of the highlights of the Mexican cultural calendar; it was founded by

students in the 1950s in honor of the great Spanish writer Miguel de Cervantes. Guanajuato provides the colonial backdrop for one of the world's great arts festivals, which brings together theater companies, dancers, musicians, and the paying public from across the world.

October/November
• *Día de los Muertos*, or *Hanal Pixan* (the Day of the Dead, October 31–November 2) is the defining Mexican festival, and certainly the most

visually arresting. It begins on the night of October 31. The belief is that the dead have divine permission to visit friends and relatives on earth once a year, and they are welcomed with offerings of food and flowers between this date and November 2. Salt and water, or the favorite meal of the dead person, may be left out for the spirit to come down and "eat." Candles and incense are burned in graveyards, and tombs are decorated with flowers, but this is no somber occasion. History has given Mexicans a familiarity with death that is perhaps beyond the usual Western comfort zone: it is both mocked and celebrated. The skulls and skeletons on display everywhere are a uniquely Mexican artifact. They are spectacular, amusing, and made of any material imaginable, from tin to chocolate.

November
• **Revolution Day** (November 20) is an official holiday. Children parade in revolutionary costumes—it's more of a ritual than a festival.

December
• **Our Lady of Guadalupe** (December 12) is the Day of the patron saint of Mexico (see Pilgrimages, below).
• *La Noche de los Rábanos* (the Night of the Radishes, December 23) takes place in Oaxaca. Radishes are carved into intricate animal and other shapes and put on display in the city's central square. Originally a gimmick to attract people to the pre-Christmas market, it must now be counted among the more original excuses ever devised for a big party.
• **The *Posadas*** (December 16–24) dramatize the journey of Mary and Joseph to Bethlehem. These are candlelit processions from house to house, the culmination of which is the smashing of a *piñata*, a colorful papier-mâché figure full of goodies. The children, blindfold, take turns to swing at it until it breaks and spills its riches.

• **Christmas Eve and Christmas Day** (December 24 and 25). As in most Catholic countries, Christmas in Mexico is celebrated on Christmas Eve (*Noche Buena*). A midnight mass is followed by a traditional supper at home, which varies, according to income, from simple corn dough *tamales* to roast turkey, ham, or suckling pig. In the capital and across the north of the country, lucky children may open their presents on Christmas Eve or Christmas Day.

SAINTS' DAYS AND PILGRIMAGES

Most Mexicans celebrate the day of the saint after whom they were named as if it were another birthday. They receive gifts and cards, and this is as much an excuse for another party as a Catholic observation.

The devout Catholicism of many Mexicans extends beyond merely attending mass on Sunday. Pilgrimages are periodically made across the country to shrines of Mexican saints.

The first and most important of these shrines is that of the Virgin of Guadalupe, now the patron saint of Mexico. The story goes that she appeared in December 1531 to an Aztec peasant, who had converted to Christianity and taken the name Juan Diego, on a hill in what are now the northern suburbs of Mexico City, the Cerro del Tepeyec. (Not entirely coincidentally, the hill was formerly dedicated to Tonantzin, the benign Aztec earth goddess.) The Virgin told him to instruct the local bishop to build a church on the site. The bishop ignored him until the Virgin appeared again; she told Diego to pick flowers from the hill and take them to the bishop, who found that the cloak into which Diego had gathered the flowers was imprinted with an image of the Virgin.

A church was built on the site in 1533, and more have been added since, each in turn housing the sacred cloak. The baroque façade of the eighteenth-century basilica makes it arguably the most interesting, but the modern, circular church built in 1976 is impressive for its scale—it  seats ten thousand and is full every Sunday. A conveyor belt in front of the framed cloak stops people lingering too long before the image.

Each year, on December 12, the second apparition is commemorated with a gathering of several hundred thousand people. In the weeks leading up to this massive religious event, groups of poor, white-smocked people move purposefully along the roads to the shrine. Some cover the last miles on their knees as an act of devotion.

"WITCHCRAFT" AND SUPERSTITION

Lumping these two headings together is a little unfair, as in Mexico witchcraft goes far beyond superstition. It should really be classed alongside Catholicism in terms of how strongly people believe in it, if not actually with regard to the number of adherents. But many believe in both traditions simultaneously: witchcraft is not a dirty word as far as Mexicans are concerned. It has more to do with healing rituals and traditional herbal medicine than with putting curses on people, although this happens sometimes as well. And it is not confined to isolated backwaters: in Mexico City's Mercado de Sonora (see Chapter 6) you will find all manner of herbs and plants for sale, most of them for use in witchcraft and healing, together with strange and exotic animals.

Well-respected witch doctors (*curanderos*) practice all over Mexico. This is particularly the case in the state of Veracruz, where, using lotions and potions, medicinal plants, effigies, charms, and black or white magic, they treat their patients for anything from ill-health to employment or marital problems. The "gift" is thought to be hereditary, stemming from pre-Columbian times.

Isolated indigenous communities still follow the shamanic beliefs of their ancestors. Shamans are a combination of doctors, priests, and healers. They regard the material and spirit worlds as inextricably linked, and in constant contact. These communities are in regular communication with their deceased ancestors, and believe that their spirits often visit the living world. One example of this  (and there are dozens) is the Huichol Indian community on the border of Nayarit and Jalisco states in the Sierra Madre Occidental mountains.

Every year Huicholes travel to their sacred mountain near Real de Catorce, an eerie former silvermining town in the distant state of San Luis Potosí, to gather the plants needed for their practices, which are found only here. Symbolism is vitally important to the Huicholes, and appears on their brightly colored yarn weavings, beadwork, and decorative containers. The three most sacred symbols are frequently depicted— corn, deer, and peyote (a hallucinogenic cactus).

Many Mexicans are superstitious, some more than others. Popular sayings refer to curses: one good example is that if someone is looking at you strangely, they're giving you *mal de ojo* (the evil eye), which brings bad luck. A particularly middle-class, urban openness to newer kinds of superstition is a more recent development. New Age and esoteric shops offer self-improvement books, palm and tarot readings, candles, crystals, and rituals for love, success, and happiness.

chapter four

MAKING
FRIENDS

Meeting people and making friends in Mexico is not as daunting as it may at first seem. The sealed, unknowable Mexican character is the stuff of legend. But although this reputation does have a basis in reality, you will find Mexicans open and hospitable once you have put in the time getting to know them, and they are not the coldest of people even on first meeting. Those used to British reserve will recognize the formal first handshake, but it soon warms up after that.

So, how do you get to know Mexicans? If you are either working or studying in Mexico, the first you are likely to meet will be your colleagues or classmates. With the former, you will soon be on friendly terms after the necessary formality of a first business meeting. Mexicans usually socialize in big groups of friends or family. Once you have made a friend, you will be accepted into his or her group, and will very quickly find yourself with a social life. But going out for drinks or dinner is one thing, and being invited to someone's home is quite another—Mexicans entertain casual friends and acquaintances outside the home, which is reserved for family and close friends.

What Should I Talk About?

A genuine interest in all things Mexican is not a bad position to start from. As in any relationship, you can gradually increase the numbers of "safe" subjects. But it takes time to feel your way, and you should remember that while a Mexican can criticize anything of his that he wants to (his football team, his mother, his country), you should never join in. This sensitivity should work both ways—if someone is unremittingly critical about your country, you should take it personally—they don't like you!

MEXICAN HOSPITALITY

Mexican hospitality is difficult to fault. The one criticism that you could make, if you were feeling particularly churlish, is that it is nonnegotiable. You are expected to accept a person's invitations, and they may be offended if you do not, especially if you are a foreigner with, it is assumed, nothing better to do. You will be expected to reciprocate at some time, although if you are only there for a short time this does not apply. If you consistently refuse invitations, the worst that will happen is that you will be labeled as someone who doesn't join in, but if you go to one party you won't want to refuse the next—Mexican gatherings are simply too much fun. The Mexicans are equally pressing and generous with food—try everything, and eat well!

Better Late ...

With regard to timekeeping, remember that a social engagement is not a business appointment. If you show up to a party at the time specified by your hostess, you are likely to find her with her hair in curlers. It is not just fashionable to be late—it is unusual not to be.

There are, of course, exceptions. Obviously you must be on time for such occasions as baptisms, weddings, and funerals. And don't ignore the significance of being invited to dinner at someone's home in a country where people tend far more to go out to socialize. Whereas you can be an hour late for a party and still be one of the early arrivals, dinner invitations are less flexible—fifteen minutes to half an hour after the specified time is probably about right. If you are invited for dinner, you probably know your hosts well enough to be able to judge when to show up.

NEIGHBORS

Given that most people in cities live in large, impersonal apartment blocks, it is not that easy to get to know your neighbors. You may share a hallway and walls, but there will be little opportunity to socialize. People seldom stop to chat in the elevator or on the stairs, though that is less true the smaller the building, and you will certainly get closer to your neighbors if your apartments are within a house. The person you will all undoubtedly know is the *portero*, or doorman, if you have one. He knows all, and generally tells all, and at the very least is a good source for finding out the gossip about your neighbors and the neighborhood in general.

EXPATRIATE ASSOCIATIONS

It is a good idea to register with your embassy or consulate, which may be able to give you a list of clubs or associations set up by people from your home country. These can vary from charitable associations to sports and special interest groups. Even if you decide to avoid your compatriots and explore Mexico's cultural riches on your own, these contacts can be a useful source of recommendations for anything, from Spanish classes, doctors, and dentists, to emergency plumbers. The realities of Mexican society, and its relative impenetrability, however, mean that you are likely to call on these contacts for more than just the basics—expatriate organizations run sports teams and other specialized clubs, and will be able to point you toward someone who shares your interests. You will be surprised by the variety of activities on offer.

SPORTS AND OTHER CLUBS

While football (soccer) is *the* national obsession, American sports feature prominently in Mexico. Baseball is probably the U.S.A.'s most successful sporting export. A significant number of Mexicans also play Major League baseball north of the border, so it is no surprise that it should be popular with locals and American expatriates alike, both to play at an amateur level on the weekends and as a spectator sport. Mexico even has its own professional league.

Joining others for sports or other common interests is a good way to get to know people, and also to practice your Spanish—it is easier to feel confident and comfortable if you are doing something you enjoy and can discuss. However, Mexico's public sports system is not great, and clubs and associations do not advertise in local newspapers, but by inquiring through any contacts you have, including your embassy or consulate, you can access a wider world of flesh-and-blood Mexicans outside the expatriate crowd.

Private clubs are a different matter. These range from small tennis clubs, through fully equipped gyms in urban areas, to large, exclusive city and country clubs that provide every kind of sporting activity and a huge bill at the end. Golf is an elite minority sport in Mexico, but there are plenty of good courses. Every beach resort has at least one, catering to rich tourists and charging accordingly. There are also plenty of courses inland, and these, especially around the capital, tend to cater to a more Mexican or long-term expatriate membership. Nearly all will allow you to arrive at any time, pay a green fee, and play. Dress codes are more relaxed than in either the U.K. or U.S.A. Tennis may not be quite as elitist or exclusive, but most courts are run by private clubs. Showing up and playing is not an option, but if you are in Mexico for long it is worth joining a club.

So good are the Caribbean reefs, Pacific waves, and limestone caves nationwide (a third of Mexico sits on limestone), that many foreigners have moved to Mexico specifically for the purposes of pursuing their passions for diving, surfing, and caving.

chapter five

THE MEXICANS AT HOME

Rapid urbanization over the last forty years has swollen Mexico's cities. In the mid-1960s roughly 50 percent of the country's population lived in urban areas. That figure now stands at over 75 percent as people have migrated to the cities to find work (or not, in most cases). A thousand people a day are said to arrive in Mexico City alone. Along with the overall high birthrate, this phenomenon has transformed the country's urban areas.

MEXICAN HOMES

The type of home a Mexican lives in will depend mainly on his or her economic status. But other factors include its location—whether in a city , in a smaller town, or in a rural area, and also which region it is in. This last variable concerns architecture and building materials rather than size. For example, the Yucatán and southern lowlands are warm year-round, including at night, and houses are therefore left more open to the elements. In the northern states, where the desert bakes in the summer and in places sits under a blanket of snow in the winter, stone is the main building material, walls are far thicker, and houses can look like fortresses, with small windows to keep the heat in or out.

More often than not, however, people in cities live in apartments and those farther out of the center or in smaller towns live in two-story houses or midsize bungalows. In more rural areas, and poorer areas of towns, families live in small one-story houses built around a central courtyard. These often house several families. Government housing schemes, which are generally built by private companies and subsidized by the government, are easily identifiable. They are mostly located on the outskirts of towns and cities and are often not particularly attractive or spacious. Uniform rows of small square houses, often with tin roofs and with tiny plots around them, stretch in long, unbroken lines, but though they may seem depressing they are at least planned, with electricity and water supplies, and provide housing for the poorer sections of society.

There is not nearly enough of this kind of housing, however, and unplanned "boroughs," ranging from newly and hastily constructed

WHO RULES THE ROOST?

The straightforward answer to this is "Mother." Mexico is a profoundly matriarchal society and maternal power rules families. It is a question of "traditional" roles reinterpreted: as men are still the main breadwinners, women are in charge of the home, and therefore the family. It makes sense. Reverence for women stretches a long way back: the country's patron saint since 1531 has been the Virgin of Guadalupe.

Mexican women as a rule are generally very house-proud, and even though an apartment complex may look neglected from the outside it will be sparkling indoors. Daughters may be expected to help around the house, but sons are not, and tend not to volunteer. Some enlightened husbands will help a little, but again that is rare.

shantytowns, to more permanent and solid developments that have grown out of earlier shanties, are a guaranteed feature of any large city. They are known as *ciudades perdidas*—"lost cities," an accurate description of a problem of which mainstream Mexican society is willfully ignorant—and are the Mexican equivalent of Brazilian *favelas*. To put it in cinematic terms, the run-down, crime-ridden Rio neighborhood in the Brazilian film *City of God* is replicated in the Mexico City *barrio* in *Amores Perros*. They are the poorest and most dilapidated areas of any town, and certainly not where you would want to find yourself on a dark night, or even during the day.

HOME HELP

Many people in Mexico, whatever their social status (apart from the jobless poor), have someone who helps out around the house. What exactly this entails can vary enormously, from someone who cleans a couple of times a week to a full-time, live-in maid. The richest families will employ a maid (or several), as well as a chauffeur, gardener(s), and a nanny for the children. Other options include masseuses and manicurists who come to the house once a week. None of these services are seen as excessive—on the contrary, if you can afford "home help," however modest and badly paid (there are so many unemployed people in Mexico that wages are low), and choose not to exercise your right to it, then you are doing society a disservice by denying people a living, or so the theory goes. In practice, the number of people you employ in your home is a status indicator, so it is rare to find people doing society that particular disservice. Even young, single, supposedly self-reliant professionals have a maid.

Generally speaking, domestic employees are treated well and will often work for the same household for long periods, frequently becoming part of the family. In richer families, a nanny may see a child through from birth to adulthood, and deep affection may be felt toward her. There is often less formality and deference than there might be in the equivalent family in the U.S.A. or the U.K.: this is one situation in which class barriers may be broken down, and an example of the Mexican respect for other people's dignity in action—in many cases, and only up to a certain point. Some families expect their employees to wear a uniform and walk a few paces behind them when out shopping.

DAILY LIFE

Daily life in Mexico is a struggle for many people. In a country where a very few are very wealthy, 40 percent live below the poverty line, and the majority are not a long way above it, this is hardly surprising. It follows from this that most Mexicans work hard: the reality of the caricatured Mexican asleep in the afternoon under a broad-brimmed *sombrero* is that he has probably been up working since 5:00 a.m. The routine described below only applies with any accuracy to the urban middle classes. Poorer sections of society tend to get up and go to bed earlier, often simply because they will have farther to travel to work every day.

Despite eating late in the evening and staying up even later, the day starts early for most Mexicans, at around 7:00 a.m. Breakfast at home is often rushed, as many people will eat a second breakfast or a snack later in the morning. For office workers, the working day begins at 8:00 to 8:30 a.m., but breakfast meetings (see Chapter 8) are common, and this is where the day's business (and eating) starts in earnest.

Lunch starts no earlier than 1:00 p.m. and generally at around 2:00 p.m. It is a more expansive affair than in the U.S.A. or U.K., generally taking two hours or more, as it is the main meal of the day in Mexico. If people can get home, they will. If they must have a meeting over lunch, the lunch is never secondary to the business at hand.

Given the longer lunch, businesses tend to be open later, but most will be closed by 7:00 or 8:00 p.m. The evening meal starts after 8:00 or even 9:00 p.m. It is lighter than lunch and will be eaten at home with the family, or out. Mexicans are friendly and sociable, but they are also reserved, and are not quick to invite people into their homes—socializing is generally done outside.

DAILY SHOPPING

Convenience shopping in large, anonymous supermarkets is not yet a big feature of Mexican life, although it is becoming that way in the larger cities. Generally, people shop for fresh produce on a daily basis in local street markets, and that is built into the daily—generally morning—routine.

Shopping is also a social occasion, with the actual transactions often seeming to be the least of it—news, gossip, and pleasantries are exchanged between shoppers and with stallholders. As you will see in Chapter 8, business in Mexico is all about personal relationships, and it is no different at street level.

LEISURE TIME

Mexicans spend a large proportion of their leisure time with their family, at home or out. As has often been said before, the family is at the center of Mexican life. Having said that, Mexicans do get away from the family now and again! Later we shall see what they do when they go out in the evenings or watch sports on weekends, but Mexicans also *play* sports.

Soccer is *the* sport. Just about every male in the country has kicked, does kick, or will kick a ball around with his friends on weekends or in the evenings. Some take it more seriously than others and there is a large amateur league structure in place. To a lesser extent, this is also true of baseball, an increasingly popular participatory sport, while American football, in the form of NFL games beamed in from the U.S.A., has inspired many to play. Women often play volleyball or go swimming.

EDUCATION

Education is very important to Mexicans. The fact that *bien educado* means both "polite" and "well educated" is no accident. Education is a means for bettering oneself. In adult life, professionals address each other formally by referring to the level of qualification each has earned: you would refer to *Maestra* Hernández if Mrs Hernández were a teacher, not *Señora* Hernández, because she has earned the qualification, and therefore the right to be known, as a teacher. Such respect for professionals, especially teachers, is rarer in the U.S.A. and U.K.

Primary Schools

Children often attend school from the age of three or four, and although preschool is not compulsory at the moment, it soon will be. There are six grades of compulsory primary (*primaria*) school, from ages six to twelve. Some schools are state-run and follow a strict curriculum, but most are private. Private schools cover a full range of options, from the quite basic to the very grand and exclusive, producing the ruling elite. All primary schools have to follow SEP (*Secretaría de Educación Pública,* or Ministry of Education) regulations, which dictate the core curriculum.

Most parents who can afford it are attracted to private primary schools by the range of subjects they offer in addition to the core curriculum. At the most basic, this involves an hour of English a week—not much, but still one more hour than in most state schools. In some states English is compulsory in all schools, state and private, although in most cases only a bare minimum of English is taught. In the more expensive private schools a significant number of lessons—ten or more hours a week, including science and math in some cases—are taught in English. These schools are called *colegios bilingues* (bilingual schools), and charge a premium.

Primary school hours are generally 8:00 a.m. to 1:00 or 2:00 p.m., with some private schools offering extracurricular activities and sports in the afternoons.

Secondary Schools

Secondary (*secundaria*) school is also obligatory for three years, up to the age of sixteen. Again, there are state (*secundaria oficial*) and private schools, and generally speaking the state schools are of a mixed standard at best.

English is a compulsory subject at secondary school. One anomaly is that even if you have studied six years of English at primary school, you have to go back to the beginning and start from the basics, as pupils' levels of English are not guaranteed. In practice, pupils are streamed into classes according to their ability.

Secondary school hours are the same as primary, although many schools also have lessons in the afternoons.

Prepa (short for *preparatoria*) is the next stage up, and involves preparing students for entry into university. This level is not compulsory, and the reality is that most young people leave at the end of secondary school (and some before that).

LEARNING ENGLISH

As will probably be apparent by now, learning English is something that many people do in Mexico, both at school and afterward. It is seen as a way of getting ahead. English is the language of international business (most foreign businesses operating in Mexico are from English-speaking countries, the U.S.A. in particular), and that spoken by most tourists in the country. So the fact that English is compulsory in secondary schools and common in many primary schools is hardly surprising, but many adults also like to learn or refresh their English, either in courses (paid for by themselves, or in some cases their company) or by talking to foreigners. This is more of an urban-oriented view, however, and people in rural areas often speak no English, and even Spanish as a (distant) second language.

TV AND RADIO

Mexico has nine television channels, two of which are state-run. Some cannot be seen across the whole country, although the two state channels (11 and 22) can. They are generally more interesting than the seven privately run channels, and broadcast cultural and scientific programs, rather than pandering to the advertisers and going for lowest-common-denominator TV—mainly American programs dubbed into Spanish, as well as the phenomenon of the *telenovela*.

Telenovelas are the Latin American equivalent of the British or American soaps. The most popular of these long-running programs are homegrown, but they may also be Brazilian or Argentinean. Interminable and unlikely as their plots are, they provide a distraction from the harsher realities of life. A stereotype fixed in the Mexican popular imagination is the housewife profoundly addicted to these melodramas, who suffers along with their characters, though it is questionable how specific this is to Mexico.

Other long-lived series include comedies, the most popular being *El Chavo del Ocho*. Other prominent items in the TV schedules are sports, wrestling, and news.

There are also a number of cable television channels in Mexico. The most popular is Cablevisión (owned by the country's largest TV company, Televisa); it is relatively inexpensive and carries a number of sports channels and mostly lowbrow American programs. Also on its signal are international news channels such as CNN and BBC News 24.

You will be able to pick up at least one local radio station in every city in Mexico. In larger cities and tourist areas, these play songs in English all day, as well as transmitting English-language programs at set times.

chapter six

TIME OUT

FOOD AND DRINK

Mexican food has a richness, fieriness, and sheer sensuality that add up to an intense sensory experience. Smell and taste are a given, but the food is also visually arresting and can even sound mouthwatering as it is prepared—there's nothing quite like the sizzle of chicken in a heavy, smoke-blackened, cast-iron pan.

Whether you find Mexican dishes pleasurable or not depends largely on how spicy you like your food, but to leave out chilies is to miss the point. However, if you are used to the bludgeoning heat of Tex-Mex food, be prepared for a pleasant surprise. Tex-Mex generally uses an excess of chilies and cumin and nothing else. It is a pale imitation of the real thing, and is generally, quite inexplicably, the type of Mexican food that is exported. Food in Mexico is infinitely more subtle and varied, although some dishes *are* hot. If chilies worry you, start off by ordering your food without them and then gradually increase the dose. But be warned—they are addictive.

Mexican food blends ingredients from the Old and New Worlds. Chilies, as well as corn, turkey, chicken, vanilla, and chocolate (to name but a few) date from preconquest times, while the Spanish introduced, among other things, dairy products, beef, wheat, onions, and garlic. Food from the north of Mexico is generally drier and served with wheat *tortillas*, small flat pancakes, while southern dishes have more sauce, less meat, and are served with corn *tortillas*. Chilies are a key feature of both traditions, which converge in Mexico City, although you will find every kind of Mexican food, as well as most kinds of foreign cuisine, in cities throughout the country. Smaller towns tend to have a more regional flavor—a slightly limited choice is more than compensated for by the freshness of the ingredients (think shellfish straight out of the sea!).

Basics

The wheat *tortilla* is just one ubiquitous component of Mexican meals (including breakfast). *Tortillas* can be hard and dry but are more commonly soft, and they mostly do the mopping-up job of bread in other countries.

Salsas, or sauces, are another omnipresent element. These include *salsa verde* ("green sauce," made of green tomatoes, chilies, and cilantro [coriander]), *salsa roja* ("red sauce," made of fresh tomatoes) *pico de gallo* ("chicken beak," a mix of finely chopped tomatoes, onions, cilantro, and green chilies), *salsa de chipotle* (smoked jalapeno peppers in a tomato sauce), *guacamole* (avocado and lime juice, probably one of Mexico's best-known culinary exports), and various pickled chilies and homemade tomato sauces. A third staple is *frijoles*, or beans, which are often mashed and "refried" (*refritos*), as an accompaniment.

Breakfast, Lunch, and Dinner

A light breakfast (*desayuno*) is eaten first thing in the morning, whenever possible. Mexicans then eat a hearty breakfast (*desayuno fuerte*, or *almuerzo*) after about 10:00 a.m., often consisting of dishes familiar to the English-speaking world, but with a Mexican twist. *Pan dulce* ("sweet bread") is the generic term for pastries such as croissants (or *cuernos*, horns), which are generally sweeter than their equivalent in Europe. Other breakfast favorites are *chilaquiles*, corn chips in a *salsa roja* or *salsa verde* sauce covered in onions and cheese, and eggs, for example, *huevos divorciados* ("divorced eggs"—two fried eggs on *tortillas*, with *salsa verde* on one and *salsa roja* on the other), and *huevos rancheros*, (fried eggs on fried *tortillas*, covered in *salsa roja*). *Molletes* (bread rolls halved, toasted, smothered with refried beans, and covered with cheese and, if you like, a variety of pork-based toppings) are a personal recommendation, but not every day— a piece of tropical fruit is probably better for you.

Lunch (*comida*) is the main meal of the day, and is eaten from around 2:00 p.m. This varies from region to region and from the extravagant six-course business lunch to a humble but tasty bean stew. (*Frijoles charros*, for example, are fresh black beans that have not been crushed—as distinct from the refried *frijoles refritos*. These are made into a stew, often with ham, and are the main source of protein for most Mexicans.)

A snack (*merienda*), may be eaten at around 6:00 p.m. to keep the wolf from the door until dinner (*cena*), which is often a lighter meal than lunch, and may be eaten as late as 10:00 p.m.

Seafood

With such a long coastline, fish and seafood feature large in Mexican cooking, particularly in coastal areas. Fish prepared *a la Veracruzana* is usually red snapper, cooked in an olive, tomato, chilie, and caper sauce. Seafood is kept simple— lemon and garlic are usually the only additions. Be wary, though, of eating fish and shellfish a long way from the coast, especially in the capital. Although you may well have an upset stomach in Mexico (often simply to do with the change of diet), it is best to avoid unnecessary risks. If you should fall ill, crushed papaya seeds are apparently a good stomach settler.

MEXICAN SPECIALTIES

A few typically Mexican dishes include *mole*, a sauce made from chilies, nuts, spices, and dark bitter chocolate. It is incredibly rich and equally delicious, once you get used to the idea that chocolate does not have to be sweet. A variant is *mole almendrado*, which is green from the almonds added to it. This sauce can be added to anything, but poured over turkey it becomes *mole poblano* (it originates in Puebla), one of Mexico's national dishes.

Another is *chiles en nogada*, which incorporates the red, white, and green of the national flag (in fact, many dishes do, but this one is known as the "independence dish"). Green chilies are stuffed with a ground beef and almond mix (red) and covered in a white walnut sauce, with pomegranate seeds sprinkled on top.

Simple Food

Uniquely Mexican components to a meal include *nopales*, the young leaves from prickly pears, called *tunas*, which can be eaten hot or cold in a salad; *huitlacoche* or *cuitlacoche*, a fungus that grows on corn and tastes better than it sounds; and *jícamas*, a thick crunchy root vegetable marinated in lime juice and pepper and eaten raw.

Simple meals include *tacos* (*tortillas* filled with cooked meat, sour cream, and a spicy sauce); *tamales* (corn dough mixed with meat, vegetables, or fruit and steamed inside corn husks or banana leaves); *quesadillas* (*tortillas* filled with cheese or other ingredients); *enchiladas* (fried *tortillas* with a variety of meat fillings, rolled up and covered in sauce); and *cebollas cambray* (barbecued spring onions and sauce in soft *tortillas*).

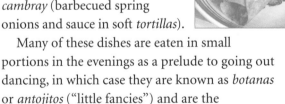

Many of these dishes are eaten in small portions in the evenings as a prelude to going out dancing, in which case they are known as *botanas* or *antojitos* ("little fancies") and are the equivalent of Spanish *tapas*.

Desserts

Mexican desserts are less celebrated, but the vast array of tropical fruit (papayas, prickly pears, *chirimoyas* or custard apples, as well as more conventional types) in the country makes up for this. Having said that, the *arroz con leche* (rice pudding, served cold) is made more interesting by an infusion of cinnamon, and the *pastel de elote* (corn cake) is an institution in the south. You will find *crème caramel* (*flan* in Spanish) everywhere.

Drinking

Mexicans enjoy a drink with their food or without it, and one drink in particular—*tequila*—has become synonymous with the country. In addition, such beers as Corona, Sol, and Dos Equis define Mexico for people who like to travel without leaving the bar. They are good, but they are not the only beers, or drinks, that Mexico has to offer. Other recommended beers include Bohemia, Negra Modelo, Pacifico, and Indio, but on a hot day nothing beats a Michelada. A mix of beer and lime juice, with salt around the rim of the glass, it is the king of shandies.

Mexican wine has not had a large impact internationally, even though the country is the oldest wine producer in the western hemisphere. Grapes are mostly grown and wine made in northern Baja California, and there are also extensive vineyards in the cooler mountains of Zacatecas. Generally, though, Californian (U.S.) red wine is widely available and a safer bet, but there are some good Mexican white wines around.

TEQUILA!

Tequila is produced from the blue agave plant, grown in vast plantations around the town of the same name. (*Mescal*, from the same plant, is often just as good, but *tequila* has to come from Jalisco state to bear that name.)

If you have tasted *tequila* outside Mexico and did not like it, it is worth giving it another chance. Mexicans drink (and revere) *tequila* in the way Scots drink (and revere) whiskey—they sip it. Not for them the slammer or hastily gulped shot to get the unpleasantness over with quickly. This is not out of masochism, but because it actually tastes rather good. Like the French with wine, they keep all the best stuff at home.

Tequila is drunk on its own, with lime and salt, as a *bandera* ("flag"—like *chiles en nogada*, this is the patriotic option, with the tricolor of the Mexican flag reproduced in three small glasses, with accompanying shots of lime juice and spicy tomato juice). If you don't want to drink it neat, avoid all the fancy cocktails and order a *paloma*: *tequila* with grapefruit juice, a splash of soda, and salt around the rim.

That said, Mexicans do not generally drink alcohol within the family, or even with friends. It is more commonly consumed at business lunches and dinners. Mexico has its own distinctive soft drinks, as well as all the global brands (known collectively as *refrescos*). *Nopal* is made from the prickly pear, *betabel* from beetroot, and the very refreshing *agua de Jamaica* from hibiscus flowers. *Limonadas* and *naranjadas* are made from freshly squeezed lemon and orange juice mixed with soda. *Aguas frescas* are fruit shakes.

As far as hot drinks go, coffee is the beverage of choice (try a *café de olla*, a combination of sweet diluted espresso and cinnamon). Tea, apart from herbal teas, is unusual. Hot chocolate is usually made with cinnamon or vanilla. The other distinctively Mexican hot drink is *atole*, made from cornmeal with milk and chocolate or other flavors.

You should always drink purified or bottled water, as water supplies may be unsafe. This is especially true of Mexico City. Some large and luxury hotels have large-scale filters, but don't bank on it. Bottled water is sold everywhere.

EATING OUT

Given the culinary riches described above, it is not surprising that eating out (or even simply eating in) is among the Mexicans' favorite pastimes, and families can frequently be spotted indulging *en masse*, especially on weekends. Individual Mexicans will eat lunch out during the week, especially if they work in an office. Small (usually family-run) café-restaurants, known as *fondas*, offer *comidas corrida*, a set three-course meal with coffee. For a decent, inexpensive, typically Mexican meal, look no further.

Cafés (in larger cities) and *taquerías* (everywhere) serve lighter meals (although it depends on how many *tacos* you have). In the latter, seating is arranged around a central cooking area: you can watch your meal being put together and pick up a few Mexican cookery tips. Eating at market stalls is also a must for more adventurous palates, but it's wise to get local recommendations first—a line is usually a good sign. Food is also served in *cantinas* (bars), but at times (in the evenings) this feels almost incidental to the hard drinking going on. Many of these establishments still bar women, or at least make them very unwelcome.

Besides the above, the country has the full range of restaurant options, from cheap and cheerful Italian to expensive and sensational Mexican, through every other permutation of cuisine from around the world. Generally, the bigger the place, the greater the choice, but you can have a spectacular meal in the smallest of towns—the key is the freshness of the ingredients. Avoid fast-food chains—they just seem wrong, given Mexico's culinary heritage.

TIPPING

In restaurants and cafés, a 10 percent tip is generally expected, but you can make it 15 percent or more for excellent service. Leave cash, and it will reach the staff concerned. If mariachi musicians play at your table, give them ten pesos, or more if you think they are worth it. At some upmarket restaurants valets will park your car—tip them five or ten pesos.

Taxi drivers don't expect a tip, but you can round up the fare if you wish. For hotel porters and doormen, a 10-peso (roughly $1 US) coin is about right, but it never hurts to be more generous.

Finally, in many cities you will come across enterprising individuals on street corners near restaurants or shopping areas who will offer to keep an eye on your car in return for a modest sum. While this is effectively a micro-protection racket, it is worth taking up their offer—five pesos is reasonable, ten is generous. "Bad things" (vandalism, say) may not happen to your car if you don't pay, but it might be safer to do so.

NIGHTLIFE

In Mexico bars are open all day and into the early hours, and besides the sometimes slightly scary local *cantinas*, larger cities have their fair share of new and modern bars, where women will feel more comfortable. Apart from drinking, Mexicans go out to enjoy live music: large and small-scale rock and pop concerts, classical recitals, *mariachi* (singing, loud brass and guitar) bands, the last often combined with an evening meal.

Theater and cinema (see below) are popular nights out in bigger towns and cities, but generally it is all about going out for a few drinks and dancing. There are large numbers of dancing establishments throughout Mexico. These play Mexican and Latin American music (*cumbía*, *salsa*, *merengue*), Cuban jazz, international pop, dance music, and many other varieties, depending on where you go.

SPORTS

The faintest of connections can be drawn between the ancient ritualistic pre-Columbian ball games and that most modern of Mexican obsessions, football (soccer), but the explanation is far simpler than that: Soccer is *the* global game. To quote the late Bill Shankly, legendary manager of Liverpool FC,

"Football isn't a matter of life and death, it's much more important than that."

As with most countries, the game began in Mexico with English expatriates, in this case Cornish miners in Pachuca in the early twentieth century, and it has grown from there. The Mexican national soccer league has eighteen teams, five of which are based in the capital. América and Necaxa are the two that share the enormous 115,000-capacity Azteca stadium in the south of the city. It hosted the World Cup finals in 1970 and 1986, and you will find a game on there or at the other two large stadiums in the capital (and at others around the country) most Sundays from August to May. The atmosphere at the big games is fantastic—the Mexican Wave was not named by accident—and generally friendly.

Wrestling, or *lucha libre*, remains popular in Mexico, especially in the capital, although it has experienced a slow decline since its heyday in the 1970s and 1980s. As with the WWF in the U.S.A., suspension of disbelief is required, as the contests are that in name only. Fans follow their heroes not only in the ring, but in spin-off comics and magazines. The biggest stars have also been featured in films. There is a political edge to the entertainment, with wrestlers such as El Superbarrio ("Super 'Hood") championing

Game Not On

During the 2002 soccer World Cup in Japan and Korea, Mexico was drawn in the same group as the U.S.A., and President Vicente Fox asked the White House whether his American counterpart would be willing to watch the game with him at a mutually convenient location on the border. He was informed that President Bush would be in bed at that hour. That hour being 2:00 a.m.

But Fox was being serious—soccer in Mexico, as in many other countries, is a national obsession, and he and 100 million other Mexicans endured agonies beyond the understanding of their largely indifferent northern neighbors when the U.S.A. won 2–0.

Mexico's urban poor and appearing at political rallies, and El Superecologista Verde doing the same for the environment. Fray Tormenta ("Father Storm"), however, is not thought to represent the Church in any official capacity. Fittingly for Mexico, all wrestlers wear masks.

Charreria (Mexican rodeo) is as Mexican as *tortillas*, and is as much a competitive sport as a celebration of horsemanship. It is popular in the northern and central states, essentially anywhere ranching is practiced. Riders compete in ten separate disciplines to the accompanying sounds of *mariachi* bands.

Mexico City boasts the world's largest bullring (Plaza Mexico, with 50,000 seats), and bullfights take place there and in other spectacular arenas in Zacatecas and Aguascalientes between late October and early April. Though hardly animal-friendly, it is a fascinating place to go and observe Mexican society. Ordinary folk watch the action from the sun-baked terraces, but also keep half an eye on the people in the seats in the shade—as in Spain, bullfighting attracts cliques of celebrities and politicians, especially when televised.

Other popular sports across Mexico include horse racing, baseball, and boxing. Many others attract minority interest, with rugby and cricket popular among British and Commonwealth expatriates, and surfing and diving among travelers and locals alike along the big-wave-endowed Pacific coastline.

MEXICAN CINEMA

Mexican cinema has penetrated the consciousness of the English-speaking world extensively in recent years. This is thanks to such films as Alejandro Gonzáles Iñárritu's supercharged *Amores Perros* (translated, somewhat lamely, as "Love's a Bitch") of 2000, which earned him comparisons with Quentin Tarantino, and

Alfonso Cuarón's 2001 road-and-teen-sex movie
Y Tu Mamá También. Deeper and more complex
work than this, such as Marysa Sistach's *Perfume
de Violetas*, 2001, is less testosterone-charged and
has had weaker international exposure as a result,
but it underlines the riches in contemporary
Mexican cinema.

The two stars of *Y Tu Mamá También*,
Gael Garcia Bernal and Diego Luna, have
been best friends since childhood, and are
currently making inroads into Hollywood.
Gael Garcia stars in a biopic of the young Che
Guevara, *The Motorcycle Diaries*, released in the
U.S.A. in November 2004, and Diego Luna can be
seen in *Havana Nights: Dirty Dancing 2*, which
came out in the U.S.A. in February 2004. A more
established Mexican presence in Hollywood is
Salma Hayek, who gave a stunning portrayal of
the artist Frida Kahlo in *Frida*.

Besides poaching talent, in recent years
Hollywood has been buying up stakes in Mexican
studios and production outfits, which has led to
fears that a vibrant, independent industry will be
subsumed into the Hollywood machinery, and
calls for a protectionist system of state subsidy.
This is unlikely to happen, but nor are Mexican
films ever going to start looking like made-for-
accountants blockbusters—Mexican culture is far
too original and strong-minded for that.

Mexico will be familiar to cinemagoers as a backdrop to recent Hollywood extravaganzas, some of them unlikely. *Troy*, with Brad Pitt, was filmed on a beach at Los Cabos, the southernmost tip of Baja California.

As for going to the cinema, English-speakers will be glad to learn that Mexicans do not dub foreign (i.e. English-language) films into Spanish, unlike in Europe. Apart from that, small independent and art-house cinemas are more common than in the U.S.A. and Europe, which ironically increases your chance of seeing an interesting film as multiplexes show a very limited range of blockbusters. Tickets everywhere are two for the price of one on Wednesday nights.

SHOPPING

Mexicans themselves don't really do shopping (it has to do with disposable income, or the lack thereof), but visitors might not be able to hold back so easily. Forget the department stores—they are the same the world over—and wander around Mexico City's markets. Buenavista is a huge hangar near the historic center containing arts and crafts stalls. Ciudadela is a smaller and more manageable covered market near the Alameda park, also for arts and crafts.

On Saturdays large bazaars are held in San

Angel and Coyoacan in the south of the city. The Mercado de la Merced, to the southeast of the center, is a huge food market. It is spectacular, but this is a dangerous place for a woman on her own. Between it and the historical center is the Mercado de Sonora, which sells items used in witchcraft. Zaragoza market, to the west of the historical center, is the city's main wholesale food market, where restaurants and hotels go for their meat, and is great for people-watching.

There is an abundance of similar markets in Mexico City and other large cities, ranging in scale from small antique stalls to large warehouses. *Tianguis* are street markets that spring up in every neighborhood once or twice a week, selling everything from fresh produce and groceries to books, household items, and cheap goods manufactured in China's vast coastal factory belt. They are rewarding places for observing daily life, but beware of pickpockets in these and every other market.

Mexican crafts are rightly world-renowned: ceramics, basket-weaving, textiles, embroidery, wood carving, metalwork and silversmithing, leather tanning, lacquerwork, and even radish-sculpting (see The Festival Calendar, p. 73) are all prominent. Around Mexico, different areas have their own specialties. Silver has been mined in the center of the country for thousands of years, and

Mexican silver is among the finest in the world. Taxco, Zacatecas, San Luis Potosí, Puebla, and Guanajuato are towns to visit for buying silver. The vast ranches in the north and west of the country have also historically provided the leather industry with its main raw material, and the industry has traditionally been based in the cities of Monterrey and Guadalajara. Other crafts are more widespread, although each region will add its own specific flavor to any given products.

CULTURAL ACTIVITIES

Mexico's cultural landscape is exhilarating. The performing arts are a rich mix of pre-Columbian dances and ceremonies with colonial and modern traditions. In addition to these and to theater and cinema, Mexico City is one of the big stops on any global tour. Major hotels constantly teem with touring philharmonics, rock stars, flamenco dancers, and myriad other performers.

Going for a stroll on a Sunday is a Mexican phenomenon that deserves to be listed under "cultural activities." It is the day when pretty much everyone is off work. Families go to the zoo (free on Sundays in Mexico City), or to green areas outside the cities for picnics, to the beach, or into city parks for walks. Diego Rivera's 1948 mural *Dream of a Sunday Afternoon in the*

Alameda in the Museo Mural Diego Rivera in Mexico City takes this most Mexican of activities and "runs with it," painting Mexican society in its entirety—historical, political, and social currents, death and sexuality, himself, and his wife of twenty-five years, the renowned artist Frida Kahlo—in one grand sweep.

Rivera was at the heart of the Mexican muralist movement of the early to mid-twentieth century, along with David Siqueiros and José Clemente Orozco. Inspired by such diverse influences as Italian frescoes, pre-Columbian art, Expressionism, and the engraver José Guadalupe Posada, who chronicled Mexican life half a century earlier, they helped define Mexico in the twentieth century, both to the outside world and to itself. Their mural masterpieces, mostly in the capital, provide a valuable insight into Mexico, as well as into how many of its people view art. They regard art as participatory, not elitist, and ordinary Mexicans probably have a greater awareness of their cultural heritage than many other nations do of theirs.

A LITTLE GAMBLING

Certain forms of gambling are illegal in Mexico, but Mexicans love a wager, on anything from boxing through cockfighting (illegal, and less and less common) to horse racing. Casinos are now being built in tourist areas such as Cancún and Acapulco, but these will be full of machines with more life in them than the dull-eyed tourists pulling on their single arms. In Mexico, gambling is, at least a little bit, about the human dimension and excitement of taking part, as well as winning.

It is perhaps because of this that Mexicans are huge fans of the different types of national lottery on offer. So it is no coincidence that the state-run lottery has been going since colonial times—in August 2004 it was 234 years old. Like the Spanish model, and contrary to the U.S. and British models where there is generally one massive jackpot winner, Mexican prize money is spread more widely and thinly, but with far better odds of winning. Rather than pick your own numbers, you buy tickets in prenumbered single units or strips of ten. The more you buy, the more prize money you get, but it will not necessarily increase your chances of winning. Maximum jackpots (and therefore odds) per ticket bought are set (from 1:10,000 to 1:25,000), which makes the draws a little more democratic and a little less random. If you can only afford one ticket, you can still enjoy the same odds as someone who has bought a strip of ten. Mass participation is therefore assured (the country spent 5.5 billion pesos on the lottery in 2002). Most Mexicans would rather go for the opportunity to make a small but significant difference in their lives than the infinitesimally tiny chance of suddenly having a fortune to squander. Essentially, Mexicans are less materialistic, and probably happier for it.

THE SEAMIER SIDE OF MEXICO

The rise of the drug cartels, centered on the border town of Ciudad Juárez, has upped the level of crime in Mexico to alarming heights in the cities. While their vast revenues are laundered through businesses that appear surprisingly prosaic, "businesses" at the seamier end of the spectrum are a secondary revenue source. Table-dancing establishments can be found in all major cities, and especially in border towns. Although some may appear more upmarket and legitimate (with names like "The Men's Room"), they are usually no more than brothels. In smaller towns such places are to be found on the outskirts and are clearly identifiable by their tackiness and flashing neon lights. As in Spain, a flashing sign saying "Club" on a (usually) windowless and out-of-the-way building denotes a brothel, not a nightclub. If you want to avoid trouble in Mexico, you could start by keeping away from such places.

chapter seven

TRAVELING

Traveling in Mexico is a hugely rewarding experience, but it is not without its discomforts. These have more to do with heat, humidity, and the sheer size of the country, rather than any human impediments, although these do play their part. On a larger scale, these include traffic and pollution in large cities and poorly maintained roads in rural areas. On an individual level, petty crime and petty officialdom are the obstacles most frequently encountered between travelers and a good time. Statistically speaking, though, you will be very unlucky if you fall foul of either of these, although you are guaranteed to be stuck in traffic if you attempt to drive in Mexico City or Guadalajara, to name but two cities.

Mexicans are religious, but this does not include censuring visitors for not dressing modestly, or for behaving "differently." This advice comes with the caveat "within reason." Beachwear should be just that—worn at the beach—but "covering up" need only involve putting on a t-shirt and a pair of shorts.

In short, Mexico is a tolerant, welcoming place in which to travel. Mutual respect is the key. If you are polite and considerate to people, they will return the courtesy, whether you are wearing shorts or a crisp linen suit.

Not surprisingly, traveling around Mexico becomes easier and quicker the more money you spend on it, but it needn't be difficult, even on a tight budget. At the top of the range, about a dozen airports welcome regular scheduled flights from abroad, and every major city is served by an internal airport at least—there are approximately sixty in Mexico. Driving obviously provides the most flexibility over shorter distances, but the country also has an extensive bus network that will get you just about anywhere, much more cheaply, though obviously more slowly, than by plane. Bus timetables and road networks are generally reliable, though this becomes less true the deeper into rural Mexico you go. Patience, fortitude, and equanimity are the attitudes to adopt when delayed, and you will rarely find a Mexican who thinks otherwise. After all, worse things can happen. And if you really aren't in a hurry, or are not too worried about where you're heading, then the romance of a train journey is hard to beat.

FLYING

Internal flights make sense in a country the size and shape of Mexico, and accordingly an integrated network of air routes crisscrosses the country, with the capital at its axis. Mexico's two main international airlines, AeroMexico and Mexicana, serve the whole country, with a number of regional airlines also covering their own particular corners, among them Aero California and AeroCozumel. Flights usually cost two to three times the price of a first-class bus fare for the equivalent journey, but can save a lot of time. Good deals can often be had by booking far in advance and shopping around. Book ahead for Christmas, Easter, and summer vacations.

Concessions and Special Deals

Foreign visitors can buy a pass, the Mexipass, before (and only before) arriving in the country and in conjunction with an international ticket (you do not have to arrive in the country on a Mexican airline), which allows them a discount on normal fares on Mexicana and AeroMexico's internal routes. A minimum of two internal flights have to be taken, within ninety days of arrival. The pass covers five different zones of the country, and how much it costs is calculated according to which zones you fly into. Travel agents will have the latest details.

BUSES

This option covers a multitude of possibilities, from air-conditioned first-class express services with plenty of space that zoom along fast toll roads, to smoke-belching relics covering local areas, in which you will be competing for space with a number of different animal species, and which are guaranteed to stop everywhere. A number of different permutations between these two extremes exist, and you can travel the country surprisingly quickly and cheaply with a bit of advance planning. Coaches (*autobuses,* or *camiones*—usually the more local buses) come in three different categories.

Luxury (*de lujo*) vehicles provide you with reclining seats, refreshments served by hostesses, restrooms, and videos, as well as the essential that is air-conditioning. These are direct intercity services (*directo* or *sin escalas,* "nonstop"), and are in theory a little more comfortable than the perfectly acceptable first-class (*primera*) services. In reality, there is little difference, as many of the first-class buses are just as fast, direct, and air-conditioned, although some will not have a restroom or a hostess. The difference is in the fares—about 25 to 30 percent. Second-class (*segunda*) services cover virtually every route in the country, but are not recommended for longer journeys, as they stop everywhere and usually have no air-conditioning. They may be the only option for local journeys, however, in which case forget about your likely discomfort and enjoy watching your fellow passengers.

All luxury and first-class, and many second-class, buses show films in English. This is not an immediately obvious benefit, but it does provide relief from the monotony of a long journey—and distances can be huge in Mexico.

Every major town has a bus terminal; some have separate terminals for luxury/first- and second-class buses. Urban sprawl and increasing congestion in larger cities have caused many bus terminals to move away from their usual location at the center of town (Mexico City has four, in the north, south, east, and west—covering those general directions), but asking for the Terminal de Autobuses or the Central Camionera will generally get you there.

TRAINS

As the road network has improved, passenger trains in Mexico have all but disappeared, but they make a gloriously impractical alternative to buses, planes, and automobiles. A small, slow, and expensive first-class-in-name-only network operates with the capital at its hub, limping along and resigned to its fate as the superhighways' poor relative. Trains leave for a handful of destinations from Buenavista station, just to the north of Mexico City's historic center. However, train enthusiasts need not be disappointed as, up in the north of the country, you can still take one of the world's great train journeys.

CHIHUAHUA-PACIFIC RAILWAY

With thirty-seven bridges and eighty-six tunnels, the authentically old-fashioned railway from Chihuahua to Los Mochis on the Pacific coast offers a hair-raising epic of a rail journey. It was built before the Panama Canal as part of a fast route across the continent, but now carries tourists (in both directions once daily) through the Copper Canyon—which is in fact a series of twenty canyons, four times larger than the Grand Canyon.

DRIVING

Driving in Mexico is mostly safe and easy, although this statement comes with a few caveats, which can be summarized as follows: know where you are going, bring a good map, and don't drive on remote roads at night. Driving within Mexican cities is also not for the fainthearted.

Unless you can combine a particular fearlessness with a high boredom threshold, you should try to avoid driving in Mexico City, as *chilangos* (as the locals are known) like to hurtle along the city's wide boulevards at high speeds on the rare occasions these are not gridlocked. The city is also enormous and bewildering, and it is easy to get lost. But if you must drive, lock the doors and keep the windows closed, especially at night. This is for safety reasons, though it could also be good for your health— Mexico City air has a few extras on top of the usual oxygen and nitrogen mix, and any filter or air-conditioning system that can get between its pungent cocktail and your lungs is to be encouraged.

The country's other large cities have a little less traffic and pollution, but the same advice still applies. Signposting is less than adequate. Once you get to know an area, you will be able to make informed decisions yourself, but seek local advice and err on the side of caution.

The Roads
Outside the cities, the country's road network is mostly very good. The main arteries are divided into three types. *Super carreteras*, or "superhighways," are the widest, at four lanes, and the fastest. They have the least traffic and the highest tolls (which can be paid by credit card).

Cuotas, "tolls," are the next step down, and have cheaper tolls. They range in quality and width, from four lanes to one, and you are likely to encounter more trucks and buses. Tolls are usually paid in cash. You can

sometimes pay by credit card, but you shouldn't count on it.

Libres, or "frees," carry the bulk of Mexico's traffic (including local), so they are invariably slower. They also run through the center of towns, and some are in bad condition, but if you are not in a hurry they can give you a better flavor of the country than rushing past on a toll road.

Speed Limits

Distances are measured in kilometers and speed limits are 110 kmph (68 mph) on superhighways and toll roads, and 40 kmph (25 mph) in built-up areas. Some *super carreteras* have a higher 130 kmph (80 mph) limit, while many single-lane rural roads are restricted to 70 kmph (45 mph). Changes in speed limits will be signposted.

Robbery

On a more cautious note, some of the most remote *libre* roads have been targeted by highway robbers and are therefore best avoided, especially at night. Very occasionally, robbery takes place on

major roads, but these incidents are rare.
Common sense should dictate what you do,
where you do it, and when, but as a general rule
try not to drive at night away from the main roads
or in large cities if you are unfamiliar with them.

Road Maps

A good map and a firm idea of your route before
you set off should keep you out of trouble. The
best maps are published by Guia Roji and the
state oil company Pemex, and are sold everywhere
you would expect: newsstands, bookshops,
supermarkets, and larger gas stations.

Fuel

Gas stations are all run by Pemex, and
fuel is the same price across the
country, apart from on the U.S. border,
where it is slightly cheaper, as it is in the
U.S.A. Europeans will find fuel far
cheaper than at home, however. As a
rule, the more remote the area, the less frequently
you will pass a gas station, so fill up when you see
one. Filling stations on *super carreteras* are also a
fair distance apart, so don't drive past one if you
have less than a quarter of a tank left. Magna (*sin
plomo,* to give it its full name) is normal unleaded
and Extra (*sin plomo*) is premium unleaded.
Diesel is *diésel.*

Rules of the Road

As with the rest of the Americas, barring Guyana, Mexicans drive on the right. The rules of the road and associated signs follow international norms, and any variations are usually attributable to language (for example, P for Parking is replaced by E for *Estacionamiento*). Other than that, you should wear a seat belt—they are compulsory—and keep an eye open for speed bumps (*topes)* and potholes in unexpected places, as well as livestock in rural areas. You should not drink and drive—like everywhere else, it's illegal—even if it seems as though others aren't holding back.

Attracting unwanted attention from the police is never a good idea, as many Mexican forces have a mixed reputation at best (although the tourist police in major tourist areas are invariably helpful and most speak English). On the road, you will encounter the Policia Federal de Caminos, or Federal Traffic Police, who will help you out if you break down and come down hard on excessive speed or drunk driving. In towns you will see the urban traffic police, the Policia de Tránsito, or even be stopped by them if you are unlucky. If you say you are a foreigner, they will either send you on your way or make it clear that you are expected to pay a fine, for which you are unlikely to receive any receipt. We would recommend discretion ahead of valor on this one.

URBAN TRANSPORTION

The nightmare of driving in major urban areas
means you need some other options. Local buses
(*camiones*) are one. In Mexico City, there are also
smaller vehicles, vans known as *peseros* (as the fare
used to be one *peso*, but with inflation it is now
more like two or three). You buy your ticket on
board. Sadly, however, with rising crime, it is best
to avoid them these days. The same is true of the
capital's Metro, or subway, especially at night.

In smaller cities and towns there are similar
vans, known either as *peseros* or *colectivos*, that
follow a set route around town, and charge a set
fare. These are buses in all but size and name, and
effectively supplement the *camión* network.

Don't hail taxis in the street. Take one at a taxi
stand (*sitio*) or telephone one from a hotel lobby.

WHERE TO STAY

The range of accommodation available to the
traveler in Mexico is immense. Hotels, motels,
hostels (youth or otherwise), historic buildings,
guest houses, apartments (serviced or not), beach
shacks, camping (free on the beaches), and even a
hammock in the corner of a beach bar: there are
options for every budget.

Mexico's hotels are graded from one to five
stars, with Gran Turismo an extra category on top

of that. In addition, historical buildings have their own special category. Some places will have no stars at all, and in every instance you get what you pay for, as the state regulates prices.

There is no lack of alternatives at the budget end of the scale. Free camping on the beaches is obviously the cheapest, though not a practical proposition in many of the larger resorts. Youth hostels, consisting of single-sex dormitories, can be found in many of the country's larger cities. Many are privately run but some are managed by the government's sports and physical activity commission and are attached to sports and recreation facilities. Inexpensive little hotels can be found everywhere, but ask to see rooms beforehand as some are gems and others downright shabby. Most reliable in this category are family-run guest houses (*casas de huéspedes*).

Mid-range hotels can be memorable, as they generally include old *haciendas* and historical buildings that have not been taken over by large hotel chains (although those that have are invariably splendidly restored—it's just that they are also far more expensive). Among chains that are reasonably priced are Presidente hotels.

At the top of the range, the hotels are often spectacular. The Camino Real chain features striking buildings by contemporary Mexican architects as well as beautifully renovated colonial mansions. International chains such as Marriott and Sheraton are also well-represented, and reliably luxurious and bland. Go for something Mexican if you can.

HEALTH

Larger Mexican towns usually contain at least one pharmacy, although this is less likely in more rural areas, and the pharmacist will be able to deal with minor health problems. Medication that requires a prescription in other countries, such as antibiotics, can often be sold over the counter. Prices are generally higher than in the U.S.A. and roughly equivalent to the U.K.

It is a good idea to travel with a small standard medical kit. Include antiseptic cream or lotion—especially useful in the humid tropics, where even a simple cut will quickly become infected if left untreated. Also bring an insect repellent lotion to rub on exposed skin. Water purification tablets should be included (but drink bottled water wherever possible), and antidiarrhea pills and rehydration salts.

Bring any prescribed medication with you, along with such items as contact lens solution or a spare pair of glasses, as necessary. The sun is scorching, and prevention is the best cure for sunburn: a high-factor sunscreen lotion, a hat, and sunglasses are mandatory.

Malaria is present in the rural south of Mexico and in up-country Yucatán, so precautions should be taken for visits to these areas. No vaccinations are required before entering Mexico, unless you are arriving from a country where yellow fever is present, but if that is the case the chances are you will have been vaccinated against it (and you will need to produce the relevant document). Visitors to remote rural areas should be immunized against hepatitis A and B, typhoid, and diphtheria, as well as polio and tetanus (you should get a booster injection for the latter).

NATURAL HAZARDS

• Coral cuts (especially from live coral heads) should be washed out thoroughly with vinegar or, failing that, your own urine, as they become infected very easily if left untreated. The same is true of jellyfish stings.

• Shake out your shoes before putting them on in the morning as scorpions (*alacranes*) and other insects sometimes crawl into them. Regarding scorpions: if their pincers are large relative to their tail (these are generally dark in appearance), they are relatively harmless, and their sting will hurt but not poison you; but beware of the pale yellow ones (*alacranes güeros*, which have small pincers, relative to their body size, and a large tail, complete with poison sac) in the dry north of the country, as a sting from these will require you to pick up an antidote from a local medical center, or suffer several hours of agony.

• The much-maligned tarantula is relatively harmless. Black widow spiders are the venomous ones—in the west of Mexico they nestle in your shoes.

• Altitude sickness is usually brought on by a quick change upward—for example, the three-hour drive from Acapulco on the coast to Mexico City, at over 8,000 ft (2,500 m), or an attempt to climb any of the country's high mountain peaks quickly. If you are attempting to walk up a mountain, regular stops will help you acclimatize and avoid unnecessary pain. If symptoms persist, the simple solution is to head back downhill. Symptoms of altitude sickness include dizziness, nosebleeds, and breathlessness. On arriving in the capital you may at first feel dizzy and breathless. The incredibly high pollution levels also play a part, but in general try to avoid too much exercise or alcohol while acclimatizing.

• Remember that the sun is incredibly strong, and that sunburn is unbelievably unpleasant. Sunstroke is worse, and can even result in death. The locals seek out shade wherever possible, and you would be well advised to do the same.

Health Insurance
Mexico's healthcare system, despite the promises (and in rare cases, the efforts) of a succession of elected representatives, remains a problem. Visitors from north of the border will probably be familiar with the reality: if you have health insurance, you will be taken care of, but if you don't and fall seriously ill, you will be in trouble. Travel insurance is indispensable.

SAFETY
Although parts of Mexico suffer from high levels of crime, it is, broadly speaking, a reasonably safe country to travel in. This statement, however, is based on the assumption that the traveler is well-informed, and if not, is following basic common sense and exercising a degree of caution in unfamiliar circumstances. A woman alone is not always safe, and certain parts of the country also come with a stronger warning. When it does occur, crime in Mexico is often violent, especially in Mexico City, and the border towns of Tijuana, Ciudad Juárez, and Nuevo Laredo. A large increase in violence in these cities over the past ten years has been blamed, rightly, on the drug

cartels, but the low apprehension and conviction rates of criminals are a significant factor. Other metropolitan areas have lower, but still serious, levels of crime.

Precautions

Overall, Mexico is relatively safe and friendly, and you would be very unlucky if any of the following things happened to you. Forewarned is fore-armed, however, so here are some useful tips:

• Abduction. Foreigners have been abducted and held at gunpoint while their bank accounts were systematically cleared out. This is especially true of Mexico City, where bogus taxi drivers pick up unsuspecting foreigners for that purpose. For this reason, it is best to take cabs from regular stands. If it happens to you, stay calm and give your assailants the relevant passwords/PINs—they are generally only after your money and will let you go once they have got all they can. Banks can afford the insurance to cover your losses.

• Similar things have happened to visitors to resort cities, who have been abducted after their drinks have been spiked. They have generally been alone; so go out in a pair or with a group.

• Armed street crime is a problem in all the major cities. Be aware of your surroundings, even in areas generally considered to be safe, and try not to travel alone, or go out alone at night, especially if you are a woman. Use ATMs during the day and at a "protected" facility (in a bank or mall).

• Pickpocketing, purse snatchings, and hotel-room thefts: take precautions. Public transportion is particularly popular with pickpockets. Leave valuables in a safe place. Make use of hotel safes when available, avoid wearing obviously expensive jewelry or clothing, and carry only the cash or credit cards that you will need on each outing.

• Try to avoid leaving belongings unguarded on the beach while swimming.

• If you are a victim of crime in Mexico, report it both to the nearest police headquarters and to your nearest consular office.

PLACES TO VISIT
Mexico City
In Mexico City—or "el DF" (pronounced *el dé éfe*)—the essence of Mexico has been distilled (some would say distorted) and scattered beneath a thick blanket of smog in a sprawling urban mass on an epic scale. It contains multitudes of people (22 million at the last count) spread over vast slums (*ciudades perdidas*, or "lost cities"), grandiose neighborhoods, and everything in between. It is the beating heart of the country in every conceivable way: politics, art, literature, music, nightlife (and even crime).

The intense energy and variety of this megalopolis will leave you giddy. Aztec ruins sit alongside magnificent Spanish baroque cathedrals, and the best view of the city (pollution permitting) is from the top of a gleaming glass and steel tower. Highlights include the Museum of Anthropology, vast murals, markets, and characterful old neighborhoods—and the city's traffic has to be driven (or sat) in to be believed.

Major Cities and Sites

Urbanization has been one global trend in which Mexico has led, with mixed results. Its cities,

however, are nothing if not varied. From the relatively clean and modern Monterrey, through any number of old, distinguished, and slightly decrepit towns and cities, to the all-encompassing vastness of the capital, they are bound to contain something to both please and appal everyone.

Every corner of Mexico has its own attractions, which range from awe-inspiring pre-Columbian pyramids to huge modern beach resorts. The following recommendations may give you an idea of where to start.

Teotihuacán is the most imposing of Mexico's countless pre-Columbian sites, and certainly the most visited, given its location just north of Mexico City.

The baroque architecture of the Spanish colonial period provides very different backdrops, depending on the location. Mexico's second city of Guadalajara is a teeming hub of popular culture, *mariachi* music, and *charreadas* (a Mexican version of the rodeo), while the many old silver-mining towns (Taxco, for example) in the country's colonial heartland provide more genteel charms.

Apart from a few pockets in the north of the country, indigenous culture is generally more apparent in the south. Oaxaca, the city and the state, is home to Zapotec Indians and a place to visit for a strong flavor of their culture.

More modern attractions include a range of beach resorts, from small, remote eco-lodges to massive, brash cities such as the world-famous Acapulco, with its cliff divers, on the Pacific coast, and Cancún on the Gulf coast. The diving is better on the Gulf side (Cozumel Island, south of Cancún, has one of the world's best reefs), while the wave-rich Pacific coast has long attracted wintering surfers from California and elsewhere.

chapter eight

BUSINESS BRIEFING

A truism of doing business anywhere is that it depends on who you know at least as much as what you know—this applies more in Mexico than in the U.S.A., Canada, or the U.K. Mexicans, in common with many other "Latin" countries in Europe and the Americas, value good personal relations extremely highly in a business context. A higher degree of contact than you might be used to is expected in order to keep the wheels running smoothly on any given project or deal. This is quite a pleasant way of doing business, but may require a certain amount of retraining.

"Hard-nosed" and "no-nonsense" approaches are not impressive to a Mexican. But abandon right now any notions of the lazy southerner as a Mexican archetype. Mexicans work hard. Those that have jobs, anyway. Those that do not often work even harder, and in an incredibly resourceful way, in order to scrape together a living.

MEXICO'S BUSINESS LANDSCAPE

Mexico varies hugely in terms of physical geography and climate, and it is no different economically. The country's industrial development has been built on the back of its oil reserves, but there is considerable diversity in the economy. The six northern states have enjoyed higher levels of investment in industry over the past fifty years due to their location on the U.S. border. In fact, the whole border area was a *maquiladora*, or "assembly plant," zone, where special tax breaks were available to foreign-owned (usually U.S.) companies employing Mexican labor, from the late 1960s onward.

The NAFTA agreement of 1994 effectively extended this zone across the whole of Mexico, at least for U.S. and Canadian companies, although industry has become more concentrated in the old *maquiladora* zones rather than spread southward. Mexico's less publicized Free Trade Agreement (FTA) with the EU in 2000 is less significant in terms of volume of trade, but will undoubtedly open up the Mexican economy to Europe (and vice versa), and might even stimulate industry away from the U.S. border zone.

At the moment, however, the north remains the most industrialized part of the country, with Monterrey as its modern heart. A roughly straight line drawn from Puerto Vallarta on the Pacific coast through Guadalajara, Mexico City, Puebla, and across to Veracruz on the Gulf coast delineates, approximately, the country's other major industrial belt. As a general rule, the further south you go, give or take a few huge empty spaces in the north of the country, the less industry there is. The Yucatán peninsula and southernmost states of Oaxaca, Tabasco, and Chiapas, as well as most of Baja California, are relatively untouched by heavy industry.

THE BUSINESS CULTURE

Working hours in Mexico vary from business to business. Many factories, especially in the northern *maquiladora* zones, are open 24 hours, in three shifts of eight. Office hours are generally from 8:00 a.m. to 6:00 p.m., with lunch usually taken between 1:00 and 3:00 p.m.

Main branches of major banks in Mexico City and Monterrey are open from 8:00 a.m. to 7:00 p.m. on weekdays (to 9.00 p.m. in some cases), and on Saturday mornings. Expect a long wait. Smaller branches in these two cities, as well as banks in most other cities, are open from 9:00 a.m. to 5:00 p.m., while in small provincial towns many banks close at 1:30 p.m.

Status and Hierarchy

Status and hierarchy are very important in a Mexican business, and in Mexico in general. This is reflected in the management style, with even mundane decisions often being passed back up the "chain of command." It is important to be aware of this, as it will help to avoid misunderstandings.

If a company you are dealing with is sending its top executives to a meeting, you will be expected to do the same. Not to do so would give a negative impression of your commitment to the deal in question. Likewise, if you are a "decision maker" yourself, you are not meeting your counterparts within a Mexican company, and progress is slow or nonexistent, the chances are that they are trying to send a message to you. Mexicans are rarely blunt in their business transactions—their approach is more "softly-softly," the idea being that you should get the message through negative "vibes" before an outright "no" has to be given.

In addition to cultivating a good working relationship with the key decision-makers, it is also important to understand the hierarchies within Mexican companies. Bosses are expected to lead, and as such are treated with deference and respect—this is all the more genuine if the respect is reciprocated and authority is not abused.

The family is paramount in Mexico, and a

person's right to a work/life balance is not in
doubt. If a Mexican employee approaches their
boss with a personal problem, it is important for
the boss to respond immediately, if only to make
an appointment to deal with it or discuss it in
more detail later. An employer is expected to at
least empathize with an employee, if not actually
safeguard their emotional well-being. The payoff
comes when there is more work to do than there
are working hours in the day—employees will be
more willing to put in whatever extra time is
necessary if they feel valued. In Mexico, basic
regard for an employee as a person is still
regarded as good management.

Nepotism

People skills and the nebulous art of "networking"
are important if you are to get ahead either in a
relationship with a Mexican business or as an
employee within it. Intelligence alone is not
enough, nor in fact are the relevant education and
experience, although they do help. The
qualifications for promotion are personal loyalty,
friendship, and ability, in that order.

Nepotism is relative. Purely meritocratic
systems, where the cream rises naturally to the top
and every deal made is transparent, whether in
business or government, are a myth in any
country, and Mexico is no different. Socializing

with the competition, head-hunting, wining and dining, gift giving, and employing the boss's friends and relatives ahead of more capable individuals are features of modern business everywhere, but particularly in a relationship-based business culture such as Mexico's.

BUSINESS STYLE

Appearance is important in a business context, and Mexicans dress formally for meetings. You should do the same. If in doubt, be conservative. For men a suit and tie, and for women a formal suit or dress, always with tights and some makeup, are the norm, whatever the weather.

If it is raining, as it frequently does in the summer months, use an umbrella rather than a raincoat, as the latter will simply be too hot. Bear in mind that most buildings in Mexican cities are air-conditioned and that you will generally find respite indoors. If the building you are in is not air-conditioned, it is perfectly acceptable to take off your jacket and even roll up your sleeves once you are settled into a meeting.

The Mexican business style is generally quite relaxed, but a first meeting will be more formal. First impressions count, so you should know at least a few words of Spanish, how to address people (see below), and what to expect.

BUREAUCRACY

There is lots of it: it is unavoidable, time-consuming, and can frustrate even the most patient of people. Patience, fortitude, and equanimity are the only attitudes to adopt.

This is just one context where building personal relationships is a real help. Contacts within Mexican business will help smooth your passage through the red tape. A lot of it is about who you know.

ADDRESSING AND GREETING PEOPLE

Mexicans have three names: their first name, their father's surname, and their mother's surname, in that order. You will see all three on a business card, or the third will be abbreviated to an initial, but you should only use the first (i.e. paternal) surname when addressing people.

Getting people's names right is a good start, but it is only the half of it. A title is a very important thing to a Mexican, and confers a certain status. These titles have nothing to do with nobility—they either invoke the bearer's academic degree, and therefore their level of education, or their seniority within a company. Referring to a professional merely as *Señor* or *Señora* Rivera (to pick a surname at random), especially in a business context, is a big *faux pas*. It is also important to get the title right. *Ingeniero/a* Rivera would be an engineer. *Arquitecto/a* Rivera would be an architect. *Doctor/a* Rivera would be a doctor, medical or otherwise (someone who has earned a Ph.D, for example—a more highly qualified academic would be a *Profesor/a*). *Licenciado/a* covers lawyers and a number of nonspecific professions, and is indicative of a bachelor's or master's degree. If someone has a title, it will be on his or her business card. If in doubt, it is better to address someone with the title you feel may be most appropriate to them, rather than simply reverting to *Señor* or *Señora*, although attaching a title to someone who is obviously not a member of the professional classes will also earn you a sideways glance.

While you are crossing this minefield, there is the simultaneous problem of how to greet people physically. Actually, this is very simple. No physical contact is not an option—at least a handshake is mandatory when meeting and saying good-bye to someone, as a diffident wave would be interpreted as rude. Men greeting men they know will often mix in a pat or two on the shoulder or back. Women meeting women will shake hands and often kiss on one cheek. In both cases this process will be repeated when saying good-bye. If you are meeting (and saying good-bye to) someone of the opposite sex, the woman should take the lead where the single kiss on the cheek is concerned, but a handshake will usually suffice when meeting someone for the first time. It is very important to get the handshake right: firm, but not overwhelming or overlong.

WOMEN IN BUSINESS

As in many other countries where *machismo* apparently endures, the myth trails a long way behind the reality. Doing business as a woman in Mexico will come as a pleasant surprise if you are expecting the worst. Warnings on the subject of personal safety in large cities and remote areas—not going out alone, etc.—certainly apply (as they do the world over), but in a business context you are unlikely to be treated with anything other than respect and acceptance. Mexico is a modern country, and the modern Mexican woman is a professional, cosmopolitan, and integral part of it. You will find many women in middle and senior management, though business remains to a large extent male-dominated. Generally, Mexican men treat businesswomen with old-fashioned courtesy.

APPOINTMENTS AND COMMUNICATIONS

Use the phone when making an appointment, as simply sending an e-mail or faxing with no other form of contact is less likely to make a positive impression. When organizing an appointment, bear in mind Mexican working hours and habits, as well as vacation periods. Christmas and Easter are particularly fruitless times for doing business, as are Friday afternoons.

If you have made an appointment a long way ahead of time, or from abroad, you should telephone again a few days in advance to confirm. Some secretaries may not speak English, so have a few words of Spanish at your disposal, or a Spanish-speaker as backup, as a secretary is very much the gatekeeper to the boss—get her (it is generally a her) on your side and you will find meeting her boss far easier. Be on time for an appointment, but don't be put out or discouraged if you are kept waiting for a while. It is not meant as a slight.

The Mexican business communication style is as you would expect: relaxed and friendly, with the all-important warm, human touches. It is advisable when sending a business e-mail or fax to a Mexican to be more long-winded than you might otherwise be. Begin with "Dear," or even "Hi," and end with "Regards," or "Best regards." Don't forget the human side on the telephone either. It's always good to ask after the family.

FLEXIBILITY AND DECISION MAKING

Time may be money in the English-speaking business world, but Mexicans are rarely slaves to the clock, and have a less regimented approach to punctuality. We have seen that this is especially true in social circumstances, where you should never turn up on time for a party—it is more a case of pathologically than fashionably late. In business situations, there will always be a good reason for someone being late for a meeting, and if it involves any combination of Mexico City and traffic, the chances are that it is true. The important thing to remember is that it is not indicative of that person's level of interest in any deal or situation, or of their "respect" for you.

Flexibility in timekeeping should be matched by flexibility in planning and decision making. Mexicans are often better at knowing what they don't want than what they do want, and one of the results is that plans are never set in stone. Decisions can be delayed or altered right up until the last minute. This *modus operandi* can save you from getting something hideously wrong by slavishly following a skewed agenda, though it can also be incredibly frustrating when you feel you have a good plan. In the latter case, keeping minutes is vital as it allows you to pin people down and keep everyone involved going in roughly the same direction.

MEETINGS

Where meetings are concerned, a rigid agenda is not the Mexican way. Instead, meetings flow, and such agenda as there is (and there will be one) follows the conversation. Topics come and go, while points are raised and dropped accordingly. Tangents and red herrings are frequent, the idea being that this will encourage a creative approach to the problem at hand. This format will be familiar to those in more creative businesses in the English-speaking world, but it is one that applies to every industry in Mexico. If you have a set agenda, bring it along and tick off points as and when you come to them. Trying to bend the whole meeting to your rigid will is futile—the best you can hope to do is steer the conversation in the right direction.

Practical manifestations of this slightly anarchic approach to meetings include people answering their cell phones, talking among themselves, and drifting in and out of the room. It is rare to have only one person talking at any time, but this is all acceptable—even necessary—behavior. If you don't interrupt negotiations, you are not likely to be heard at all.

If you are making a presentation you can expect a little less chaos, but don't be surprised if

conversations break out. Given all of this, it is
probably no accident that many business meetings
take place over a meal, where the format is less
restrictive.

Business Breakfasts

These are frequent affairs, and although they take
place in a restaurant, they are closer to a meeting-
with-food than the more social and expansive
good-meal-and-a-good-chat model of the
business lunch. They can take place at any time in
the morning (generally starting between 8:00 and
11:00 a.m.), and will be fairly short, sharp affairs,
rarely lasting more than an hour and a half, where
specifics can be discussed and paperwork is
spread across the table.

Business Lunches

Lunch is the main meal of the day in Mexico, and
this has shaped the format of the business lunch.
It begins between 2:00 and about 4:00 p.m. and
can go on into the early evening (so keep your
afternoon clear in case!). It is a full meal, with at
least three courses, and is usually about getting
acquainted, sizing each other up, and deciding
whether or not to do business together, at least in
the early stages of a business relationship. It is
important to realize that what you are doing is
more than just talking around the subject and

wasting time: you are building and cementing a relationship. As a rule, Mexicans will do business with you only if they feel they know you, like you, and can trust you. Lunches are about the "big picture," not the minutiae of any given deal, although at more advanced stages in negotiations, deals are often closed over lunch.

Business Dinners

Dinners are different again, and rarer if both sides of a business deal are in the same city on a more permanent basis. Foreign clients or partners on shorter visits from abroad can expect to be entertained in the evenings. Mexicans are nothing if not hospitable, and will not countenance any notion of you languishing in a hotel, even if that is what you may want to do after a long day (if so, keep it to yourself!). If you are on a short visit and are an early-to-bed person, you should catch up on your sleep before you go to Mexico, as you are guaranteed to be well looked after and dinner rarely starts before 9:00 p.m. (and can go on until the early hours). Unlike a working breakfast or lunch, however, a meal in these circumstances should be treated more as a social occasion and you should unwind (if not actually unravel). Alcohol is served more often at business lunches and dinners than at social gatherings with friends.

Etiquette at Business Meals
Avoid initiating work-related conversations at dinner. You are also not expected to maintain "shoptalk" for the duration of a working lunch or even breakfast. Meals may turn out to be the most productive part of your day, however—as your host gets to know about you and your family, and you about his, a personal bond is established and business, hopefully, flourishes.

In these and any other social or near-social encounters, and at the risk of stating the obvious, it is worth remembering that Mexicans are fiercely proud of their country, and are generally more conservative than Western liberals—stick to safe topics. Any denigration of Mexico, even if it relates to the undeniable traffic or pollution problems, runs the risk of causing offense. A good parallel would be with your mother or sister: *you* can be rude about them if you want, but you will always bristle (or worse) if others do the same.

In terms of paying for each of these meals, splitting the bill is not really done in Mexico. In general, the party who initiated the meeting (i.e., made the invitation) pays the bill. In cases of confusion, do not offer to pay just your share—pay the whole bill or keep quiet.

One final part of business entertaining you can expect as a visitor to Mexico is for your host to show you around the local area and interesting sites. Given the importance of building personal relationships, you should use this as an opportunity to do just that, as well as to explore a beautiful country in the company of an expert rather than just a guidebook.

GIFT GIVING

Gifts are not usually given at a first meeting, but once this is out of the way and a second meeting is arranged, they can serve as a sign of a willingness to take things further. Gifts can also be given at the end of successful relationships.

Thoughtfulness rather than material value should be applied in selecting a gift. Something too extravagant may be perceived as a bribe. Instead, bring something from your own country—single malt whiskey, English gin, French brandy, European or Californian wine, or at least something not readily associated with Mexico (silver, or arts and crafts, for example, are not appropriate). Chocolates are always safe if you are really stuck. A gift with your company logo on it is too impersonal, unless it is very discreet or specially commissioned.

If you are invited for a meal at a Mexican home, chocolates, something sweet for dessert (such as pastries, or a cake), or even a simple bunch of flowers would all be perfectly appropriate. A six-pack of beer would not!

BRIBERY AND CORRUPTION

In the bad old days, doing business in Mexico used to be about tapping into a network of patronage and connection that was as arcane as it was unauditable. Bureaucracy was a nightmare, or it was not, depending largely on how willing you were to play the game and work with a system that those who fell foul of it might have described as corrupt. "Globalization" and its manifestations in Mexico, in the form of NAFTA and other free trade agreements, have not removed all the bureaucracy, but have certainly made it infinitely easier for foreigners to do business in the country.

The Mexican business community is now resolutely outward-looking. Depending on which industry you work in, and which part of the country you are attempting to do business in, things have changed or are changing. This is not really quantifiable, but at the very least Mexico is addressing the issue with an earnestness and determination that would put many a complacent first-world country to shame.

CONCLUSION

In business, as in most areas of Mexican life, the importance of personal relationships cannot be overstated. An initial formality is expected, but this should quickly give way to a more personal, informal approach. Dignity and a certain sobriety should be maintained, however—mutual respect is the key to building trust and therefore a successful working relationship.

Mexican business is all about multitasking and flexibility—different issues are dealt with simultaneously, not separately, and you will be expected to work in the same way. This is easier when others around you are similarly minded. Maintaining good relationships with both colleagues and subordinates will go a long way toward ensuring success. Contacts are crucial—if you are well thought of by the right people, you are well on your way: your product or service will be more favorably viewed once your business partners accept and like you as a person.

chapter nine

COMMUNICATING

LANGUAGE

Spanish is the official language of Mexico, and the first language of the vast majority of Mexicans. Like several other European languages, Spanish stems from Latin, but has also adopted many words from other languages, including Arabic words inherited from Spain's eight Moorish centuries. In Mexico, such borrowing has extended to the country's indigenous languages, especially in place-names.

Spanish varies, in terms of accent and dialect, from country to country. While there are differences in pronunciation and local vocabulary, a Spaniard will be understood in Mexico and vice versa. Castellano, or Castilian, began as a dialect spoken in inland northern Spain, and became the language of the court of the kingdom of Castile and León in the twelfth century, and of Spain as a whole in the fifteenth century, when the kingdoms of Castile and Aragon were united. It thus became the language of all new territories discovered and claimed on behalf of the crown of Spain by Christopher Columbus and his successors. Mexico's future as a Spanish-speaking country was all but assured when Columbus's lookout first sighted land (a small island in the Bahamas that Columbus chose to call San Salvador, in honor of his Holy Savior) in the early hours of October 12, 1492.

In most parts of Spain today a "c" followed by a soft vowel (e, i), or a "z" followed by any vowel, is pronounced with a "th" sound. Mexicans will pronounce it with an "s" sound (e.g., a *cenizero*, meaning "ashtray," would be a "thenee*thero*" in Spain but a "senee*sero*" in Mexico). Historically, Spain also used this "s" pronunciation, but a divergence occurred in the sixteenth century when the court of Charles V, the first Habsburg king of Spain, who reigned for forty years (1516–56), chose to adopt the king's own pronunciation. (The unfortunate monarch had inherited the unusual Habsburg features—he had an underbite, and an enormous chin, and was unable to close his mouth properly—and consequently spoke with a lisp.) The colonies across the Atlantic were far enough away not to have to follow suit. Bizarre but true.

Speaking Spanish
Spanish is one of the easiest foreign languages for an English-speaker to learn. Even if you only

acquire a basic knowledge of Spanish, using it will demonstrate that you have an interest in the country and its culture, and it will be greatly appreciated. Don't be shy—practice is the way to improve. The basic grammar is straightforward, and nobody will mind if you make mistakes. In tourist areas, locals will often be able to speak English, but elsewhere even stumbling Spanish will open up the possibility of better communication and understanding.

Other Languages

Off the beaten track, you may come across people who speak one of the country's sixty or so indigenous languages as a first language, or, more rarely, as their only tongue. The most widespread are Nahuatl (the language of the Aztec, with 2.5 million speakers) and Maya (with 1.5 million).

FACE-TO-FACE

Mexicans love to talk. Their Mediterranean heritage also means that they talk with their hands, though not as much as their cousins back in Spain. They will also not pay much attention to conventions of "personal space" once they get to know you. This closeness, combined with talking loudly and gesticulation, can initially seem aggressive, but it is certainly not meant to be. In a formal situation, voices will be slightly lowered and gestures more restrained.

Mexicans, in most situations outside the family and close friends, always use the formal word *usted* for "you." The plural is *ustedes*. Because this is short for *vuestra merced*, "your honor," the verbs are in the third person form. The informal *tu* uses the second person form, as would be expected, but *vosotros* (second person plural) is never used in Mexican Spanish—they will find it highly amusing. In Spain, *usted* is used less. It is a sign of respect and good manners when addressing older people or business associates in a formal meeting.

Once you have built up a friendship or a business rapport with a Mexican, there are few taboo subjects, but initially it is safer to stick to topics of general interest rather than ask a lot of personal questions. Complimentary remarks and inquiries about the local area will always get a conversation going, and you will soon find points of common interest to discuss. As mentioned before, if a Mexican is talking negatively about his country, culture, or soccer team, don't join in!

ENGLISH-LANGUAGE PUBLICATIONS

These are not as numerous as they once were, certainly in the capital. The *Mexico City Times* and *The News* were once published in the capital and employed many expatriates, but neither exists now, although *The News* is rumored to be making a comeback. Nowadays the *International Herald Tribune* is the one daily newspaper in English on sale, though many U.S. (*New York Times, Miami Herald*) and some British papers are available in the larger cities a day late. Weekly international news magazines such as *Time, Newsweek,* and *The Economist* are also widely available, as are all manner of lifestyle magazines.

Areas with large English-speaking expatriate populations, such as Guadalajara (*The Colony, Guadalajara Reporter*) and San Miguel de Allende (*Atención* and *El Independiente* are its two weekly papers), have their own weekly English-language papers. Others include the *Cuernavaca Lookout,* the *Baja Sun,* and the *Ojo del Lago* ("Eye of the Lake") in Chapala, which advertises itself as the paper of "the largest English-speaking community living outside Canada and the U.S. today," perhaps forgetting Britain and the rest of the Commonwealth.

SERVICES
Mail

Main post offices (*oficinas de correos*) are open from 8:00 a.m. to 8:00 p.m. Monday to Friday, and

8:00 a.m. to 3:00 p.m. on Saturdays. Most of these offer a mail-holding service. Letters should be addressed to the recipient at the *Lista de correos*, followed by the name of the town and the state. You will need to show ID when picking these up.

It is best not to rely too much on the Mexican postal service, and it should be avoided for sending and receiving larger packages internationally. Incoming parcels and sometimes even letters can be held up indefinitely at the customs stage, and outgoing mail often disappears long before then. In any case, fax and e-mail have supplanted most written communication, and international couriers have filled the gap left by the inadequacies of the postal system where larger packages are concerned. If you are in business, you can get a preferential business rate from various couriers (DHL, UPS, etc.), but individuals sending one-off packages will not be stung too badly either, and it does at least guarantee that a package will reach its destination.

Travelers wanting to ship goods home can look up the air freight divisions of various international airlines, or even land/sea freight companies (slower, equally reliable) for larger volumes or smaller budgets.

If you do want to send a postcard, mailboxes

are a newish shade of bright red (in Mexico City and tourist resorts) or, more commonly, yellow.

Telephone

Probably because of the inadequacies listed above, but maybe simply because Mexicans like to talk, the telephone is the most popular means of communication. However, this does not make it easy for the visitor, at least initially. The country's code is 52. Most numbers in Mexico have eight

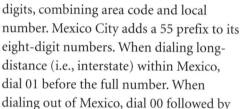

digits, combining area code and local number. Mexico City adds a 55 prefix to its eight-digit numbers. When dialing long-distance (i.e., interstate) within Mexico, dial 01 before the full number. When dialing out of Mexico, dial 00 followed by the country code. For operator service, dial 040.

There is widespread use of cell phones. Most people use pay-as-you-go telephones (Movistar and TelCel are the main companies, and the rates are reasonable compared to the U.K.). You can purchase these and buy units of call time in branches of Samborn's, among other places.

Landlines have not been completely supplanted, and local calls remain cheaper on private or public telephones. The latter are either telephone booths on the streets (easily recognizable blue TelMex telephones, known as LADATEL), which take phone cards in denominations of 20 to 100 pesos, or coin-operated phones in restaurants and shops. Both options are far cheaper than calling from hotels, especially overseas.

Mexicans say "*Bueno*?" (which roughly translates as "Well?") when answering the phone, and then wait for you to speak.

Internet

Internet cafés are widespread in Mexico (all major cities have them, as well as many small towns in more tourist-oriented areas), and they are also cheap (12 to 20 pesos an hour is typical). But connections are sometimes slow.

CONCLUSION

Upon arrival, you will soon discover that the Mexicans are a unique people. Outwardly reserved when dealing with strangers, they soon become relaxed and friendly once they get to know you. The unknowable Mexican is a myth. There is enough common ground for mutual understanding and friendship to develop.

The first reference point is family. Family life is the focal point of Mexican society, and children are seen, heard, and doted on. Wider society and its authority figures are often regarded with suspicion (often with good reason), and rules and laws are often regarded as constrictive. These, especially in the south, are often bent or ignored when expediency dictates it, although this does not mean that Mexicans lack a moral compass, or even that there is one definitive Mexican mind-set. However, a common culture—as seen in the country's festivals and *fiestas*, arts and crafts, and cuisine—is still immediately apparent to anyone who visits Mexico, as is a strong religious faith, a specifically Mexican Catholicism that borrows heavily from pre-Columbian traditions. It all adds up to a special, diverse, and provocative people.

Business travelers may well encounter delays and changes to plans. But flexibility and the personal touch are the Mexican way, and you will be pleasantly surprised by how smoothly things run once you adopt this attitude. Your Mexican counterparts are sure to be friendly, hospitable, and interested in you as an individual. Once they get to know you and therefore value you, your business has a much better chance of flourishing.

Whatever your reason for coming to Mexico, knowing more about Mexicans and their culture will help you to make the most of your time there, and also to have realistic expectations. Above all, it will help you feel more at ease in a country that at first sight may appear forbidding and utterly different, but which holds infinite riches, variety, and fascination for the visitor.

Further Reading

Azuela, Mariano. *The Underdogs.* New York: Random House, 2002.

Clendinnen, Inga. *Aztecs.* Cambridge: Cambridge University Press, 1995.

Cortés, Hernán. *Letters from Mexico.* New Haven, Connecticut: Yale University Press, 2001.

de las Casas, Bartolomé. *A Short Account of the Destruction of the Indies.* London: Penguin Classics, 1992.

Díaz, Bernal. *The Conquest of New Spain.* London: Penguin Books, 1969.

Esquivel, Laura. *Like Water for Chocolate.* New York: Anchor Books, 1995.

Greene, Graham. *The Power and the Glory.* London: Penguin Books, 2003.

Hamnett, Brian. *The Cambridge Concise History of Mexico.* Cambridge: Cambridge University Press, 1999.

Lowry, Malcolm. *Under the Volcano.* London: Penguin Books, 1969.

Maher, Patrick. *Mexico Handbook.* Bath: Footprint Handbooks, 2000.

Milton, Jane. *The Practical Encyclopedia of Mexican Cooking.* London: Hermes House, 2002.

Paz, Octavio. *The Labyrinth of Solitude, The Other Mexico, and Other Essays on Mexico.* New York: Grove Press, 1983.

Pierre, D.B.C. *Vernon God Little.* London: Faber and Faber, 2004.

Fuentes, Carlos. *The Death of Artemio Cruz.* London: Penguin Books, 1979.

Rulfo, Juan. *Pedro Páramo.* London: Serpents Tail Publishing, 2000.

Rulfo, Juan. *The Burning Plain.* Austin: University of Texas Press, 1971.

Thomas, Hugh. *The Conquest of Mexico.* London: Harvill Press, 2004.

Spanish. A Complete Course. New York: Living Language, 2005.

In-Flight Spanish. New York: Living Language, 2001.

Fodor's Spanish for Travelers (CD Package). New York: Living Language, 2005.

Index

Acknowledgment

I would like to thank Siân Hughes for her invaluable help and expertise in researching this book.